Breakthrough

THE

POWER OF THE

INTERRUPTED RELATIONSHIP

TONY HUMPHREYS
& HELEN RUDDLE

Breakthrough
The Power Of The Interrupted Relationship

First published in 2019 by
Panoma Press Ltd
48 St Vincent Drive, St Albans, Herts, AL1 5SJ UK

info@panomapress.com
www.panomapress.com

Cover design by Neil Coe
Artwork by Karen Gladwell

ISBN 978-1-784521-59-2

Printed and bound in Great Britain by TJ International Ltd, Padstow, Cornwall

Testimonials

The principal theme of this spirited book is the realisation that couple conflict is not about what happens between partners but what is happening within each of us as individuals.

Interruptions are viewed in a metaphorical way in the context of our life stories.

We never truly love another person unless we are equally involved in loving ourselves.

The book points out how we never cease to love ourselves and how our loving wisdom is always present whether we are thriving or striving.

What I like in this book is knowing and experiencing such love consciously can be our deepest quest in our human experience.

It is a book I will keep coming back to as already I've referred to it several times, a book full of soul that will have a place on my night stand for a long time.

The book articulately demonstrates the potential for all breakdowns to become major breakthroughs into the fullness of our uniqueness.

Caroline Coughlan
Practice Administrator, Awakenings Unlimited – Centre for Psychotherapy, Mentoring & Education
Midleton, Co. Cork

This book resonates strongly with me, providing a very deep and profound understanding of the meaning and purpose of interruptions that inevitably occur in our intimate couple relationships. Rather than looking at interruptions literally and seeing them as problems, they are viewed in a metaphorical way and seen as having meaning in the context of our stories with roots going back to our earliest relationships. The focus of attention then is not on what is happening between us but on what each of us is bringing to the relationship in terms of our inner worlds. This paves the way, when safe holding is present, for the opportunity to break through to a deeper, more openly loving relationship with ourselves and out of that to a real intimate connection with the Other.

The book gives us very clear waymarkers on the path to this breakthrough, guiding us in a compassionate and holistic way in reflecting on our relationship with ourselves and in taking charge of making that relationship openly loving.

On reading this book I have a sense of awe not only on how we always look after ourselves in the best way we can given our level of safety, but also on the extraordinary power of the interrupted relationship for breakthrough into the fullness of who each of us is in our unique, precious and sacred presence in this world.

Lorna McCarthy
Parent & Relationship Mentor,
Irish Association of Relationship Mentors
www.iarm.ie

This is an extraordinary book in which the authors hold the frailty of our human psyche with (in) such care and tenderness.

There is a wise parenting to this book by the authors which allows the reader to feel utterly safe to explore 'relationships' from a non-blaming place of utter compassion for both herself/himself and the Others in their lives.

This book is a love story to the Self, it is never blaming but offers instead kind compassionate wisdom to understanding our own inner creativity in surviving the fractured relationships we encounter in our lives. It teaches us that our own protective strategies are there at our own service, to help us survive the pain and loss of our relationships.

There is nothing about this book which is a practical guide to fixing relationships, but rather a call to our own individuation; a coming home to ourselves rather than seeking 'home' through others.

I cannot imagine anyone reading this book who wouldn't find it a rare, enriching experience to come face to face with their own loving nature. This book offers us a pathway to conscious love.

Dr Owen Madden
Psychotherapist at the School of Life, London

Contents

Introduction

A deep longing that we all share is that for intimate, loving connection with another, and there is no doubt that the experience of intimate connection brings great joy, warmth, a sense of aliveness, excitement and a sense of freshness, a sense of possibility in life. But the road to conscious, open intimacy is not easy; it is a road that, though we want so much to travel on it, is very often fraught with fear – an early learned fear of doing the very thing that leads to intimacy, which is to be openly and fully our unique selves.

It is a strange and extraordinary paradox that it is in taking the risk of entering into an intimate relationship that there occurs the very re-enactment of old threats and fears that provides the opportunity for resolution in the here and now of those old threats and fears. Because we always bring the story of our earlier relationships into our adult relationships, the road of intimate relationship is always going to be paved with interruptions. But those interruptions are the powerful messenger of what has had to lie hidden of your unique presence, and are the portal to breakthrough to open emergence into the fullness of who you are.

In this book, when we use the term 'relationship interruption' we are referring to the reactions of Others whereby it becomes threatening to express your individual presence. It becomes threatening to stay spontaneous, to stay real and be truly expressive of your feelings, thoughts, needs, beliefs, values, and your felt experience of life. These reactions of Others that pose threat to the expression of your individual presence lead you, wisely and lovingly, to hide those aspects of your presence that you learn are too dangerous to show.

For example, if you as a child were treated as 'stupid' by a parent or teacher, it would be too dangerous for you to contradict these powerful adults in your life, and too dangerous for you to uphold the truth of your wonderful natural intelligence. You would then wisely hide this aspect of yourself. There are myriad ways, ranging from severe to minor, in which the emergence of our true selves can be interrupted; for example, aggression, passivity, neglect, abandonment, rejection, comparisons, invisibility, diminishment, overprotection, violence, favouritism and criticism.

None of us escapes the experience of relationship interruptions. As human beings, from the moment of conception, we live in a relationship world. Depending on the nature of those relationships – depending on the extent of protectiveness present – we will feel more or less safe about giving expression to a fundamental truth; this truth being that each of us is a unique, sacred and precious presence in the world. Even as tiny infants we know when there are threats to our presence, and in our wisdom we find ways of protecting ourselves, our various and wonderfully creative protective strategies constituting what might be called a Shadow Self. The interruptions we experience in our relationships with Others become internalised as interruptions in our relationship with ourselves.

Our protectors are wise and loving but, because created in early life, are held in the unconscious – it would be too painful for us as children to face consciously the suffering we experience through relationship interruptions. The key challenge for us as adults is to bring into consciousness what has lain hidden in regard to the suffering experienced and the protectors created in response. These protectors are our powerful ally, being created to keep the suffering manageable and, very importantly, to keep the issue alive until such time as there is sufficient emotional holding to face directly what needs to be faced.

When we come into adulthood and enter into intimate couple relationship, we bring with us the story of the relationship interruptions we have experienced to date – early-life interruptions being of particular significance. Bringing into consciousness the story of the threats you experienced and the consequent protective strategies you created is crucial to your wellbeing in the here and now, and is also a key waymarker on the road to real intimacy with the Other. Story is central to the examination of present interruptions. When you have the emotional holding to consider the interruptions you encountered as a child to your natural emergence of Self, the breakthroughs that can gradually occur include seeing how powerfully and creatively you protected yourself in the face of the protective words and actions of parents and other significant persons, and how the very reactions you exhibited and continued into adulthood are the portal into all that you had to hide.

There is also the breakthrough of knowing that the threatening actions of all these adults in your earlier life were, in fact, their survival responses to the threats they encountered when children. Compassion arises for yourself as you reflect on your story, and when you begin to have a conscious sense of a solid interiority, compassion also arises for those adults whose protectors were sources of deep hurt, and gave rise to the terror of expressing the wonder of your unique presence.

The amazing thing is that our adult relationships – particularly intimate couple relationships – create the environment in which the story of our suffering and consequent protectors gets re-enacted. The power of that re-enactment is that it provides the opportunity in present adult life to bring into the light of consciousness what has had to lie hidden and to put in place now the openly loving responsiveness being called for. Taking the example above of an early relationship interruption around expression of intelligence: suppose as an adult you now find yourself in a relationship where, in reaction to this early interruption, you hide your intelligence and defer to the Other in all things to do with your shared life. This will inevitably cause interruption in the present couple relationship. You will experience all the unease and anxiety of being dependent, and the Other too is likely to feel the pressure of being the 'intelligent one' in the couple, and both of you will miss the joy of meeting the real substantial Other.

But there is the deeper reality that every interruption offers the opportunity to break through to what you dare not do or say; this hiddenness crying out for you to seek the safe holding that will enable you to come out of hiding, that will enable you to find your own solid interiority and be true to yourself and live your own precious life. The interruption could be very powerful if you can find the safety to reflect on what is happening, to begin to understand yourself, to make the link with your early-life experience, to see the protectors you have created, and to recognise and bring forward the fundamental truth of your wonderful innate intelligence. In this way the interruption can bring about breakthrough – breakthrough to the Real You who is strong, capable, in charge, resourceful.

Safe holding is crucial to release the power of interruptions to become breakthroughs. If it is interruptions to the free and spontaneous expression of our presence that lead us to create walls to hide behind, then it is open, unconditional love, and the experience of being accompanied and held wherever we are, which paves the way for gradual emergence of our true and unique Selves. Safe holding involves non-judgment, understanding, respect, compassion, kindness, responsiveness. When we are in the midst of a relationship interruption, it is often necessary to seek the required safe holding outside the couple relationship. Ultimately, we need to find the safe holding within ourselves – we need to find the safe haven within, from where we need never again suffer rejection, abandonment, neglect, diminishment or invisibility. Safe holding enables us to hold with the truth of who we are: unique, sacred and precious presences in the world, unconditionally deserving of love.

When an interruption occurs in an adulthood intimate relationship, the temptation – the protective response – is to focus on what is happening between the two people. But when this is the focus, no breakthrough can occur; what is happening between you is the outcome of what is happening in the interior world of each of you, and it is this interiority that has to be the focus. You need effectively to take your eye off the Other and look inwards to where all the important information resides. The one relationship really calling for your attention is the one with yourself – all else follows from the nature of the intimacy with yourself.

Reflecting on your relationship with yourself, and taking charge of making that relationship openly loving, is a major challenge, but it also carries a sense of freedom and relief as this is something you can do, as opposed to the powerlessness of depending on the Other to do it for you. It is not that any adult goes into an intimate couple relationship with the intention of being a source of threat – emotional, social or physical – but the reality is that a life that is unexamined becomes a life unlived and leads to interruptions in the relationship. Where the couple have children, the parents' unexamined lives go on to seriously interrupt their children's emergence. All this, of course, happens quite unconsciously. So many adult relationships are about a mutual 'mend my life' but the conscious relationship is, in the words of the poet Rilke, "where each appoints the Other the guardian of their solitude", thereby encountering the uniqueness and individuality of the Other, which always enhances one's own sense of fullness.

Our aim in this book is to guide you through this extraordinary, awesome and powerful passage from the unconsciously held suffering expressed in relationship interruptions to breakthrough into conscious wholeness. With this passage, intimate relationship becomes about being fellow-travellers, being soul-mates rather than partners in an unconscious dependent dance, being mutually supportive and encouraging of each other in the emergence from hiddenness into the fullness of who each of you is in your unique presence in the world.

In the last chapter, we also consider an even more profound breakthrough to a deep spiritual longing within us that no relationship with the Other can meet.

Chapter One

Breakdown To Breakthrough

Waymarkers On The Way To Breakthrough

There are many challenges to be faced when you choose to travel on the path to intimacy with the Other. Sadly, in our different holding worlds – home, community, educational settings, work, leisure and religious settings, and society – we do not receive much guidance on the nature of this path and what real intimacy entails. Nor are we given any real understanding of the meaning and purpose of the relationship interruptions that inevitably occur. Without such understanding, we are deprived of the power that interruptions have to lead to breakthrough for each of the two individuals involved and, consequently, deprived of the possibility of deepening the intimacy between us. Below are outlined what we believe to be some of the key waymarkers that can facilitate us in reaching what we yearn for in an intimate relationship with another.

The Impact Of The First Couple Relationship

We are always in relationship from the moment of conception. The first couple relationship we experience is with our mothers and later on, following birth, the second couple relationship we experience usually is that with our fathers, whether he is present or absent! Given that there are over 40 different kinds of family unit in the western world, the first relationship may be a surrogate mother and, following birth, an adoptive mother. Similarly, when infants are abandoned, orphaned, given up for adoption, fostered, the 'new' parent(s) may be male or female. Whether the parents are male and female, two females or two males, the essential issue is that the particular parent nurtures the feminine and masculine natural qualities of each child – male or female.

But the reality is that a parent can nurture in each individual child only what she or he is consciously nurturing in herself or himself. For example, a male parent who is, unconsciously, hidden in his emotional expression and receptivity cannot provide the safe holding for a son or daughter to express what is true of their nature – their heart side and inward side (right brain) – the wellbeing emotions of love, tenderness, compassion, empathy, warmth, kindness, joy, excitement, and the emergency emotions of fear, depression, anger, sadness, guilt, loneliness, hunger and thirst for love and recognition, hurt, disappointment and rejection. Similarly, when, say, a female parent, during her early years, has had out of fear to repress the wonderful masculine and outward qualities (left brain) of confidence, sureness, risk taking, natural curiosity, drive, ambition, firmness, solidity – all head, outgoing qualities of our nature – then this parent will, unwittingly, block the emergence of these qualities in a son or daughter.

The nature of these early parental relationships will determine how much of the fullness of your true, unique and powerful presence you will reveal or mask. Later on, other significant adults become part of your story, and you part of their story – childminders, playschool teachers, grandparents, aunts, uncles, primary and secondary school teachers, neighbours, clergy. It is accurate to say that it takes a world to raise a child, and any adult who has any degree of affirming or threatening influence on a child's life has potential impact on that child's story – whether or not the adult realises (real eyes) that possible impact. The future of society always lies with adults – not with children as is often believed – because when adults secretly have fears and doubts about themselves, children struggle to survive and, on the other hand, when adults are fearless and secure, children thrive.

Indeed, the early couple relationships between each parent and child, and the children's witnessing of their first adult-adult couple relationship – the one between their principal carers – powerfully and critically influence all subsequent couple relationships. When the nature of these highly significant relationships is threatening in nature, their impact stretches right into adulthood, and unless realised, will remain a continuing obstacle to an openly loving relationship with Self and an enriching couple relationship. The Jungian psychoanalyst James Hollis[1] put this very well when he wrote: "What remains unconscious in the parent, however well intended the parent is, is what will be transmitted to the child and remain a continuing obstacle to a fuller life." Hollis could have also said that what is unconscious in other significant adults in children's lives – most importantly, grandparents, childminders, pre-school, primary and second-level school teachers – will be transmitted to the child and, again, the child's unconscious reaction may remain a continuing obstacle

---

[1] Hollis, James. *Finding Meaning in the Second Half of Life*. New York: Gotham Books, 2006, p.136

to a fuller life. The following quote from Jung[2] reinforces this message: "What usually has the strongest psychic effect on the child is the life which the parents have not lived." Again, we would include here the effect on children of the unlived lives of the other significant adults in their worlds.

We Are Always Creative

We agree with Jung on the threats posed for children by the unlived lives of parents and other significant adults, but we see that we are never victims of what turns up in our lives; we are always active and creative agents in our relationships, albeit often at an unconscious level. When we see ourselves as victims, we have resorted to an unconsciously devised protector in the face of threat. When we realise our creativity, we have chosen a consciously formed response in the face of threat. This does not mean we do not acknowledge that we have been at the receiving end of the Other's protectors, such as violence, aggression, sexual violation; on the contrary, we assert that threat very definitely. The difference between being reactively the victim and proactively the creator is that, in the latter response, we will take the necessary actions to safeguard ourselves but will not diminish, label, judge or condemn the person who perpetrated the violations.

When we adopt the victim response, we will judge, blame and condemn either ourselves or the Other, but we will take no action to safeguard ourselves. When we blame the Other, we may retaliate with protective actions such as reciprocal violence, criticism or withdrawal. When we blame ourselves, we may beat ourselves up internally and recreate within our

---

[2] Jung, C.G. *The Collected Works.* 20 Vols. Trans. R.F.C. Hull. Princeton: Princeton University Press, 1973, 17, para. 84

interior world the very external world of physical, emotional, intellectual and social threats that we have encountered since our early days. The wisdom of such introjected behaviour is that it reinforces our defences; by making sure we remain diminished within, we eliminate risks of acting in any ways that might draw the Other's threatening responses upon us.

All of this happens unconsciously and is truly amazing – not problematic or pathological as often seen – in that it effectively buries what is inexpressible. The critical difference between the unconscious and the conscious response is that, with the former, you are looking and waiting for the perpetrator to take responsibility for the threats posed, which leaves you on very shaky and insecure ground, while with the latter you are taking active responsibility for the safeguarding of your wellbeing.

It can be seen that the most common reaction that occurs between people is the unconscious one, and unless that becomes conscious, human misery is perpetuated. It helps to remember that while we may have had to bury the truth of what we deserve and the truth of our power to safeguard our wellbeing, the truth is buried, not wiped out. In our loving wisdom we always want that truth to emerge and we are always seeking the safety that will let it emerge. When we have learned great fear about acting from the truth of who we are, we need the safety of a non-judgmental and unconditionally loving relationship with another in order for us to find the inner safety that will enable us to let the truth emerge; that other may be a relative, a teacher, a friend, a medical doctor, a psychotherapist, a mentor. When you experience safety, then what is unconscious – buried, hidden – breaks through, becomes conscious, reveals itself, and the same intelligence and creativity that went into devising your protective survival strategies can now be employed to thrive, to go from dependence to independence, from hiding to emerging, and from an unlived to a lived life. Consciousness brings about the building of bridges that foster connection with the Other, rather than the protective walls that hide the parts of ourselves we dare not show and from which we cleverly disconnect. As James Hollis[3] describes it, life now becomes a creative play rather than a means of self-validation.

The Conscious Relationship Is The Fulfilled Relationship

In order to experience a sense of real love and fulfilment in our relationships, we need to bring into conscious awareness those survival strategies that we unconsciously created in our early lives and brought into adulthood, so they do not continue to colour our way of being with ourselves and with the Other.

Our concept of what love is, and what we look for in our couple relationships, can often reflect unconscious unfulfilled longings rather than an open view. It is rare for love to be experienced as having no hidden agenda, to be experienced as awe response in the face of the unique presence of the Other, and for coupledom to be seen as being about two people. Each bringing their fullness to the relationship, whereby each appoints the Other as the guardian of their own solitude and togetherness with Self. This kind of coupledom is rare because it is not often recognised that it is the relationship that is consciously examined that is the relationship lived, and there are not many opportunities for the raising of consciousness.

[3] Hollis, James. *The Eden Project. In Search of the Magical Other.* Toronto: Inner City Books, 1998

There is a widespread notion that if the two people are 'right for one another' then it should all work out naturally without having to do any 'work' on the relationship. We do not see that there is 'work' involved in finding the fulfilling, openly loving relationships that we long for and deserve; the idea of having to work on a relationship has a heaviness, a dreariness to it and can put us off going on the path of intimacy with Another. But something very definitely does need to happen, and that something is the emergence into consciousness – the breakthrough – of what lies hidden in the unconsciousness. While there are huge challenges involved in making the shift to consciousness, it is a process that carries with it the promise of discovery, adventure, aliveness and realness – a more exciting prospect than 'work'.

There is no doubt that the conscious relationship is the openly loving, fulfilling relationship. Consciousness is the secret to being fully alive and, consequently, of being fully present to Another. Hiddenness in the relationship is an unconscious response to experiences that have had to be held below conscious awareness because they have been too threatening to face directly. The breakthrough into consciousness of what has lain hidden frees you to respond openly and straightforwardly to whatever has arisen in your story. Consciousness is liberation, is freedom; with consciousness, you are no longer weighed down by unresolved experiences from the past, you can live in the here and now. With consciousness you are freed from the 'voices' of old – voices that belong to the suffering of others – you can hear your own true voice now, the voice that knows the truth of the wonder and glory of who you are in your unique presence in the world.

With consciousness, you are no longer operating in the dark; things are brought to light – a lovely phrase and very apt in this context. Consciousness opens up possibilities, brings choice rather than being driven. Consciousness goes hand-in-hand with understanding, and understanding opens up your heart; an open heart gives energy for responsiveness, for living life to the full.

Being Together With Yourself: The Crucial Breakthrough

A central theme of the book is that aloneness is fundamental to our human nature. But, rather than this being a tragedy, we see it as offering you the possibility of standing alone, being independent and finding that interior solidity from which you can withstand, in a non-judgmental way, the unconscious attempts by others to place responsibility for their lives on your shoulders. We see aloneness as 'all-one-ness' – being together with yourself. When in our earlier lives we unconsciously realise that it is too dangerous for us to be at one with ourselves, we cleverly project that need on to others, hoping that the relationship with them will fill the emptiness within. When, inevitably it does not, we re-experience the fear and abject disappointment of earlier childhood abandonments.

Central to open, fulfilling adult-adult relationships is the realisation that, whereas when children we necessarily depended on the important adults in our lives to unconditionally love and believe in us, here and now in our adult years only we can fill that void within. But that is something we can actually do, and something for which we have all the resources we need. We have the head and we have the heart that enable us to find the unconditionally loving responsiveness that is being called for at any particular time.

When we continue unconsciously to fill the void from without – through, for example, relationships, work, sex, success, addictions to alcohol, food, the approval of others – then we remain in the childhood place of dependence; no real joy or fulfilment is now possible.

When as adults we unconsciously look to Another to fill the void within, the relationship now is arising from fear, a fear that itself arose initially from lack of unconditionally loving relationships with the significant people in our earlier lives. When you are relating from the void, the underlying fear is: I'm not at all sure that I'm going to be OK in the world; I fear I don't know how to take care of myself; I have never experienced, and so have never learned, care; I'm not at all sure that I'm even worthy of care. There is now huge insecurity driving the movement towards relationship, and this insecurity gets protectively expressed either as "I will live my life for you" or "you must live your life for me."

The unconscious hope underneath both protective responses is that the Other will do for you – love and care for you – what you are terrified of even trying to do for yourself. The result is a protective dance rather than a relationship. Such a dance can help you survive for a while until the cracks begin to show as it becomes evident that the dance does not fill the void, it does not provide a sense of security. Resentment, disappointment, punishment, withdrawal, aggression, diminishment begin to come into the interactions between you and the Other. You are blind now – to yourself and to the Other.

When you are more together with yourself, there is an underlying security that you know how to be there for you – how to give yourself head and heart care. You consciously know the truth of who you are and what you deserve – the truth of what is worthy of you. What drives the movement towards relationship now is attraction, interest, fascination in the amazing particularity of the Other. This openness gets expressed as: "My wellbeing matters and I take ownership and responsibility for its safeguarding; your support and encouragement in that safeguarding would be profoundly appreciated. Your wellbeing matters and I'll do my utmost to lovingly support and encourage you in your taking ownership and responsibility for the safeguarding of your wellbeing." Now you have real relationship between you and the Other, you have the bridge that is solid, with two sturdy supporting pillars on either side, both of which stand out in their own right. Now you can have seeing and being seen, individuality, fellow travellers, togetherness on the quest, space for co-creation.

Everything That Comes From The Other Is About The Other

A realisation that can be challenging is that everything that comes from the Other in the relationship with you is about the Other and for the Other. Each of you in the relationship is continually revealing yourself in your words, non-verbal behaviours, actions, preoccupations. Most often, the revelations from one partner come from the unconscious and are read by the other partner also from an unconscious place. While this state of play continues, your knowing of the Other on the path with you will be clouded, superficial, unreal, unsatisfying, distanced. True intimate knowing becomes possible when you, and your partner, have the breakthrough that everything that comes from the Other is about and for the Other – nothing to do with you, 100% about the Other.

With this breakthrough, you will have the safety to support and encourage the Other to go beneath the surface, unconscious revelations to the underlying truths – to what has been unsayable and undoable up to now and that needs to be brought into the light of consciousness. For example, when the other person in a relationship with you withdraws, is aggressive, manipulative, controlling, dominating, argumentative, eternally dissatisfied, needy, dependent, absent or possessive – all the foregoing being interruptions – none of these behaviours is about you, the recipient, but 100% about your partner! Let us examine this notion further. For example, your partner complains:

◗ "You're never here when I need you"

◗ "You don't listen"

◗ "You think you're always right"

◗ "You're aggressive"

◗ "You don't love me"

Let us now take each of these statements as being all about the Other – in psychoanalytic terms known as projections – and look for the hidden 'I' messages, the unsayable, coming from the Other. An opportunity now arises for you, the recipient, to get to know your partner (the sender) more intimately and, even more importantly, for the sender to get to know himself or herself more fully. It helps to see the word 'complain' as metaphorically revealing what the sender needs to do but is unconsciously fearful to do and that is to 'come plain', be clear, be open about what lies within. It is not for you to read the Other's mind – that would be taking responsibility *for* him or her and be counterproductive.

But an opportunity for breakthrough for the Other can be created by you when you can enquire patiently and with interest: "How is it that you are saying that?" There is, of course, a strong possibility that a defensive retort will be given – "Don't give me that psychological claptrap" – but then one patient enquiry by you is rarely enough for the Other to find the inner safety to say what is *really* going on for him or her. If you manage to remain separate and not personalise the retort and, once again, with kindness, say: "I would really like to hear what is going on for you," a bridge of safety may open up for the Other to realise – to become conscious – that he or she needs to speak about himself or herself and not about you.

A breakthrough may emerge that in this relationship it is the Other's responsibility to Self and to you to let you know what goes on inside him or her and to speak from the place of 'I', the 'Real Me'. Taken this way, the complaints – the protective walls – may now be revealed as the clever protectors of what the Other really wanted to say, but dared not, owing to a hidden fear of rejection. Possible unsayables creatively hidden in the above messages are:

- *"I'm never here* for myself"
- "I don't *listen* to me"
- "I need to *believe* in what I say"
- "I need to be *expressive* of what I would like in my relationship with you"
- *"I don't love me* and I'm wanting you to do the loving for me that I need to do for myself"

The Way To Breakthrough Is Paved With Metaphor

It may be that your response to the complaints above takes the form of 'surely all the Other is doing is expressing unmet needs in the relationship, and what's the point of being a couple if it's not about a mutual meeting of needs?' Touché! But it is the indirect way that the sender of the message communicates that spills the beans about deeper unconscious issues that are attempting to surface. Realisation that there are deeper underlying unconscious issues enables the interruptions in the relationship caused by the complaints to become powerful and creative opportunities for the deepening of the relationship within the sender, within you the recipient and between the two of you. Magical! Yet we so often miss the magic when we respond to conflict literally. Literalism is probably the greatest unconscious block to understanding conflict and to breakthrough – personal, interpersonal, familial, societal, educational, political and spiritual.

When you view conflict metaphorically, what is really going on becomes *clear* and the bridge to true engagement with Self and the Other appears. Somehow, a society that has become so scientifically and technologically driven has lost sight of the immense creativity of the human mind and the predominantly symbolic nature of human behaviour. Certainly, science now acknowledges that most of our behaviour is unconscious, but still struggles with the metaphorical language of the unconscious, a language that wonderfully communicates what needs to be said, but dare not be said directly, and what needs to be done, but dare not be done overtly. It is only when safe holding worlds are created – where individuals live, learn, work, play and pray – that consciousness will emerge and all that has lain hidden will be revealed.

The couple relationship offers such a possibility, and in the light of this the power of attraction to the other makes metaphorical sense. If, in the face of the unlived lives of the significant adults in our childhood years we creatively found ways to protect the pearl of great price – our unique and sacred presence – by creating a Screen Self, it makes sense that it is through conscious relationships in adulthood – relationships that provide safe emotional and social holding and that are empowering – that we can create the possibility of emergence of our Real Self. No one wants to stay hidden, and the urge to emerge will pursue us to death's door (as will the urge to merge with the Source of all that exits – more about that later).

Where You Are Is Where You Need To Be

A further realisation that can open up possibilities, and that can lead to compassion for the Other and oneself, is that where you and your partner are right now is exactly and creatively where you each need to be! Any suggestion that either of you is mad, bad, wrong, or irrational will result in a heightening of the protective walls already present. Any labelling of a person's behaviour – whether threatening or, indeed, affirming – is being judgmental, and judgment represents a serious interruption to relationships. A genuine enquiry as to how it is the Other is speaking or acting in such protective ways may evoke an unexpected response that speaks of what has been up to now unsayable and undoable. No person wants to be deliberately unkind or threatening; the number of times, over the years, we have heard clients genuinely voice "I didn't realise what I was doing" bears testament to that reality.

Recall that the unconscious protection of projection, which can create a serious interruption to the relationship in which it occurs, is designed to reduce threat, not create it, but when the person at the receiving end of the projection is also in a defensive place, that is precisely what it does. There is a double, albeit unconscious, wisdom in the foregoing, because the perpetrator's projections and the recipient's introjections often re-enact the very threatening behaviours that interrupted each person's emergence in their earlier years. The unconscious hope is that the truth of what happened will finally come out into the open. Most importantly, the protective responses are powerfully, albeit covertly, designed to offset the recurrence of the worst blow to one's presence: abandonment in the various forms experienced. Taking the person where she or he is right now, and recognising the wisdom of the interruptive responses here and now, are the most important steps to creating a bridge that connects you with the Other and an opportunity for a deepening of relationship within and between you both.

Each Couple Has Its Own Particular Path

Each couple relationship is unique, involving two individuals coming together who each bring a unique presence to the Other along with their unique life stories. Furthermore, what is unconscious in each partner has been uniquely fashioned and will be transmitted to the Other, and what is transmitted unconsciously will be received unconsciously, unless the Other is consciously grounded in Self and separate. When the unconscious worlds of two partners clash, the relationship between them becomes interrupted. The depth, breadth, intensity, frequency and endurance of the interruption are determined by the nature and level of the hidden and unresolved abandonments experienced within each of them. No two couple relationships are the same, and the resolution of any interruptions will always be unique in nature.

Interruptions arising from the unconscious inner worlds of each partner can present in a myriad of ways, usually the two partners coming from opposite positions, as in the examples over:

Partner A	Partner B
Always in	*Always out*
Passive	*Aggressive*
Frequently ill	*Overburdened*
Compliant	*Dominant*
Enmeshed with family of origin	*No time for family of origin*
Addicted to caring	*Work addicted*
Addicted to rescuing	*Helpless, waiting to be rescued*
Silent	*Forcefully vocal*
Appeasing	*Hypercritical*
Inferior	*Superior*
Clinging	*Elusive*
Cowed	*Demanding/commanding*
Martyr	*Narcissist*
Emotionless	*Histrionic*
Hidden	*Pushy*
Malleable	*Manipulative*
Frightened	*Threatening*
Perfectionist	*Careless*
Pessimistic	*Unrealistic*
Detached	*Jealous*
Emotionally withdrawn	*Possessive*
Anxious	*Depressed*
Miserly	*Extravagant*
Makes heavy of everything	*Makes light of everything*
Joyless	*Giddy*
Turned off sex	*Sex addicted*
Very private	*Gossips*

No matter what the troubled and troubling behaviours expressed by each partner, these behaviours, paradoxically, are portals into what lies hidden and are crying out to emerge. It is not what is visible but what is invisible that needs to be the focus of attention.

Considerable emotional holding is required for breakthrough to occur, but be assured that whatever relationship interruption may be present, this has been unconsciously but creatively and cleverly designed for resolution of all the unsayables and undoables that have been hidden within up to this time.

Chapter Two

What Is This Thing Called Love?

What Is Love?

Your notions of what love is will be heavily influenced by your experiences of relationships to date. If relationships have been relatively openly loving and unconditional, then you will be able to look on love with clear eyes. But if, as is most often the case, your experiences of love have come with conditions attached, then you will necessarily look on love through the shadow of protective strategies such as introjection and projection.

The challenging aspect of figuring out what love is all about is that virtually all relationships start out not from conscious clarity but from unconscious introjection and projection. We come to adulthood with a view of love that springs from childhood experiences that were most often experiences of protective rather than unconditional love, and that in turn led us to be protective in our expressions of love. Once these unconscious protectors are present, they unintentionally, but nonetheless powerfully, interrupt what we really want to express – unconditional love. Both introjection and projection reveal interruptions to relationship that have occurred in our earlier lives, and are continuing in the present.

Examples of some typical, annihilating introjections are: 'I feel like nothing'; 'I am nothing if I don't have a child'; 'I hate myself'; 'I'm useless'; 'I feel worthless'; 'I just want to hide away.' Less severe introjections are: 'I feel so confused'; 'I don't like anything about myself'; 'I feel stupid'; 'I don't have what it takes to make a relationship work'; 'I dread waking up'; 'I worry about everything'; 'I feel so ugly'; 'I hate my body.' You can see that if you are in such a state of fear that such protectors are necessary, it would be just too risky for you to open up to intimacy with another.

Examples of highly threatening projections are: 'You are my world'; 'You must only be there for me'; 'Success defines me'; 'You only think about yourself'; 'You hate me'; 'Nobody wants me'; 'I'm sorry I ever met you.' Less threatening projections are: 'You disappoint me'; 'Without family, I'd be lost'; 'You never listen'; 'You're insensitive'; 'You're driving me mad'; 'You're so aggressive'; 'You're a mouse.' Again, it is easy to see how the level of fear underlying such projections would make intimacy out of the question. Both introjections and projections can be communicated verbally, non-verbally – tone of voice, facial expression, body posture and movement, eye contact – and through actions; for example, dismissal, silent treatment, self-harming, violence towards another, self-neglect and neglect of others.

In childhood, when our adult carers manifest introjections (blame themselves) and projections (blame the children, other adults, the world, God), these adults are unconsciously transferring their relationship history on to us, their children, whose stories are just beginning. This is the nature of the human condition; nobody is to blame, rather what is called for is understanding and compassion. But it needs to be acknowledged and understood that once our childhood natural emergence is interrupted, then we, in turn, begin to create our introjections and projections, and the whole sad saga is repeated. Of course, in most cases, some glimpses of what love truly is are experienced, particularly where the protective strategies of the adult carers are not impenetrable. For anyone who experienced severe interruptions to the expression of their individual presence, such glimpses will be few and far between or even non-existent.

Whatever the level of protective response, we suffer as children because consistency and predictability of love are not present, and the experience of that loss gets carried into adulthood, until the time comes when there is sufficient safe holding for that pain to break through into conscious awareness so that it may now be resolved. Intimate relationship with another has the potential to provide just such safe holding, this being one of its greatest powers.

Parents can bring to their children only what they see in themselves – if I am blinded by fear, I cannot see myself nor can I see the Other. Even with the best will in the world, the parent who protectively sees himself or herself as useless, stupid, unlovable or ugly will not be able to see the natural capability, intelligence and beauty of his or her child. Likewise, the parent who has not had the safety to follow his or her own dreams and hopes for life will either disempower the child through projected anxiety about the world – 'best to stay with what you're used to'; 'do what everybody else is doing'; 'you might regret it later if you change direction now'; 'follow the rules and you'll be all right' – or will load the child with his or her unfulfilled longings, directing the child on to a particular path, or pushing for achievements that are not necessarily what the child wants for himself or herself.

The child, of necessity, takes on the image of himself or herself projected on to the distorted mirror held up unconsciously by the parent and begins to hide his or her natural light and radiance. But it is crucial for our wellbeing as adults that we do not stay stuck in protective blame of our parents and other carers, but instead begin to find now the open, straightforward, unconditionally loving responsiveness for ourselves that our parents in their suffering were not able to provide for us. We need to be mother and father to ourselves, and to the extent that we can manage to do that we will have fulfilling relationships with Others now.

When it comes then to adult meeting adult, when one psycho-social story meets another psycho-social story, each will unwittingly transfer their hidden suffering on to each other. What is clear from this is that the quality of each adult's relationship with himself or herself will totally influence the quality of relationship with the Other. No matter whom we are with, or where we are – family, school, workplace, community, church, sports and leisure settings – we bring with us how we see and feel about ourselves. Real progress in making connection is not possible unless we come into consciousness of the nature of our particular psycho-social stories, and the resultant relationship with ourselves that we have developed.

Love can be openly and truly present only when we are conscious. The well-intentioned love that we wish to communicate to others – children, partners, friends, colleagues, clients – can so often be ambushed by our highly developed unconscious protectors. You may, for example, love your life-partner dearly, and at the same time find yourself being protectively possessive and controlling out of a hidden fear that you may not be enough for him or her, and that there is a danger again of being abandoned, just like in childhood. The question arises as to what the experience of unfettered conscious love would feel like. If it is true that we cannot bring to another what we have locked away in ourselves, surely it is equally true that if we see the good in ourselves, we will also see the good in the Other.

Conscious love is being in touch with our own individuality, our fullness, our power beyond measure, our uniqueness and unrepeatable potentialities, and from that solid interiority seeing all that too in the Other. Such love reaches out to the heart, mind and spirit of the Other and, most importantly, can see through the walls of protectors to all the glory that lies hidden behind them. There is now unequivocal cherishing, non-judgment, belief, compassion, understanding and awe. Naturally, the boundaries are present that are required for conscious safeguarding in the face of the threats to wellbeing that are posed by the protective words and actions of Others. The operative word here is 'conscious' so that in establishing boundaries – caring actions for oneself – there is no lessening, judging, labelling or diminishing of the Other.

When the light of your conscious love is present, the potential for a raising of consciousness in the Other is greatly increased. Of course, raising of consciousness is the Other's own responsibility but is more likely to emerge when there is enduring love, patience and belief coming from you. When Others in our lives get any sense that our expression of love for them has a hidden agenda of changing them, they will intuitively batten down the hatches in the face of such conditionality. The impulse to change the Other is unconscious; the change we wish to see in the Other is the conscious emergence that needs to happen within ourselves!

If conscious love is an emergence that needs to be realised for all adults, what is the particular thing about intimate couple love? We believe that coupledom is important for children, not only for the sharing of the sacred responsibilities of caring for them and enabling them to care for themselves, but also so that children can have the experience of expressing their dignity, power with and independently of their parents, and feel confident of generalising that experience to other significant adults in their lives. Furthermore, a couple can model for children what conscious couple intimacy is all about. But intimate coupledom is not just about creating a safe environment for children; it is primarily about the particular potential for the full and open emergence of Self that resides in the intimate sharing of one's life with Another.

But the potential for emergence in intimacy, which can be usefully read as 'in-to-me-see', can often be side-tracked by the unconscious unfilled hunger for love experienced by many adults – a hunger for that unconditional love they did not receive as children. The fundamental need to love oneself is projected on to a potential lover, that she or he will do for you what you are fearful or terrified of doing for yourself. Unconsciously, we hope that the person we are attracted to will fill the emptiness within and, as many of us have experienced, we will go to the ends of the earth to achieve that protective goal. The extremes we can go to include aggression, passivity, self-abnegation, possessiveness, jealousy, paranoia, violence, self-harming, attempted suicide and, when rejected, even murder or suicide. None of these reactions (creations!) are evil (which, interestingly, in its letters, is the inverse of 'live') but rather are the tortured behaviours of unrequited love.

Kahlil Gibran,[4] when asked to speak of evil, responded with these profound words (the bracketed words are ours):

"Of the good in you I can speak, but not of the evil. For what is evil but good (love) tortured by its own hunger and thirst. Verily, when good (love) is hungry it seeks food even in dark caves, and when it thirsts it drinks even of dead waters.

You are good when you are one with yourself. Yet when you are not one with yourself you are not evil."

Our search for love outside of ourselves reveals our fear of us loving ourselves. The most common plea we hear, not only from clients but from friends and professional colleagues, is: "How do I love myself?" The plea does not suggest that we do not know how to love – we are too intelligent and creative to not know. No, the reason for the plea is that loving ourselves is something that we dare not do because of a life-story that made it threatening to openly do so; to allow ourselves to become conscious of the fact that in our own hearts we do know how to love ourselves requires a high degree of safety and so, wisely, we seek a *substitute* – somebody to do it for us. But there is no substitute for the real thing!

Nonetheless, without the substitute of a lover, a friend, a marriage partner we would likely plummet into despair or find other substitutes, such as alcohol, food, drugs, work, success, physical fitness, some obsession that will temporarily fill the unrequited longing within, until the time – whenever – we realise that the person for each of us is 'Me' and was there

---

[4] Kahlil Gibran. *The Prophet.* Macmillan edition. 2015, p.77

all the time with the longed-for love. This awakening does not come easily but the possibility is always there and, we believe, each one of us wants to become 'one with ourselves'.

It seems then that the intimate relationship with Another is unconsciously created with the sole purpose of unearthing your own Real Self and of you seeing into your Self (in-to-me-see). It may seem paradoxical, but it is when that dawning occurs that the possibility of real connection with Another begins. Furthermore, as consciousness rises, appreciation of and compassion for the suffering of the Other will emerge, as will the readiness to support him or her in the journey of self-discovery and self-realisation.

A question that often arises is: when I find intimacy with myself and enjoy my own aloneness, will I really need the company of an intimate Other? The answer to that question is that I will always want connection with Others; the experience of loving connection with Another – even if only passing – is the most profoundly joyful experience we can have as human beings. We live in a relationship world and the more those relationships are real and unconditionally loving, the more the suffering we experience in our human existence is reduced. But the reality is that there is only one route to real connection with another and that is real connection with oneself.

When I am at one with myself, I will recognise my desire for loving connection with another, and I will have the safety to pursue that desire in an open, straightforward way. I will be able to see the Other as a fellow-traveller, distinct as a presence in their own right, rather than as the medium for the filling of an inner void. The challenge is huge – finding your own fullness, all-one-ness – but when two individuals can meet in the fullness of who each is – knowing and being fully known, receiving and being fully received – then there is deep joy, a sense of rightness, of lightness.

What Is Falling In Love About?

What has 'falling in love' got to do with love? The answer to that question comes when we investigate the felt experience of 'falling in love'. The experience typically comprises a confusion of welfare and emergency feelings. On the one hand, it feels wonderful to be in love, the world appears bright and beautiful, you feel bright and beautiful but, on the other hand, the experience is also fraught with anxiety – you find yourself looking for evidence of continued interest from the Other – insecurity – will this last? Jealousy and possessiveness – is someone else attracting his or her interest? Pressure to present an unreal image where you have no faults, shortcomings or irritating habits. The welfare feelings indicate that there is something good happening here and, of course, there is: the good thing being the experience of attraction and that you are getting a glimpse of what it might be like to be in intimate connection with Another.

The emergency feelings reveal the hidden fears and challenges that are involved in actually following through on that desire to be intimately connected with Another; the central challenge being to find your own loving connection with yourself and the fear that surrounds finding self-connection. Fear is the ground of the falling-in-love experience, that fear leading to projection on to the Other as the source of your sense of lovability and power to attract. It is not uncommon for two people to start out being madly in love with one another, not wanting to be apart for a moment, only for one or other to declare at some later stage "I'm no longer in love with you" as if this were something that just came over him or her, and that provides the perfect rationale for leaving the relationship. But falling out of love has its own unconscious reasons, just as has falling in love, and unless these unconscious reasons come to light, the person is likely to go from one falling in love experience to another without ever finding the self-realisation that leads to abiding love with Another.

Fascinatingly, the term 'falling in love' secretly captures the projection in the experience. When we 'fall' we let ourselves down, and 'falling in love' represents the 'mis-take', the failure (the fall) of believing that the Other is going to fill the void within. Many of the 'in-love' song lyrics reinforce the projection – for example, 'I can't live if living is without you', 'you were made for me', 'you are the sunshine of my life', 'you're my everything.' The 'you' refrain puts all the responsibility on the Other's shoulders to 'mend my life' and when the Other declares 'I'm no longer in love with you', it 'rends my life'.

The hidden issue within the 'in love' experience is that I am needing proof of my lovability and I am putting the proof totally in the Other's hands. When the Other accepts this dynamic, there is now a co-dependent relationship that is seriously interrupted from the outset. It is no wonder then that the bitterness that is evoked when the dream does not come through – when the void within is not filled by the Other – manifests in such outbursts as "I can't stand the sight of you" or "I feel nothing for you" or "I don't know how I could have been so blind", "I should never have married you." The partner at the receiving end of such harshness inevitably suffers hugely so long as he or she does not yet see that the Other is talking totally about himself or herself. The 'I can't stand the sight of you' reveals how the Other has not got sight of Self; the 'I feel nothing for you' shows how invisible the Other is to Self; the 'I don't know how I could have been so blind' exposes how blind the Other is to his or her own presence; the 'I should never have married you' reveals the lack of marriage with Self.

Of course, at this stage, neither partner is in a conscious place to realise the profound wisdom of the painful conflict. The pain being about the absence within each of them of a loving relationship with Self, and the conflict – the blaming, the withdrawing, the aggression – being a path for each of them to come home to themselves. It is a relief, even if a huge challenge, to realise that being, rather than 'falling' in love with Another is about a reciprocal bringing of our fullness, not our emptiness, to the Other. It can happen that a couple who truly love each other's presence may choose to part because of significant differences in values, life choices, beliefs and attitudes, but they will do so amicably and support each other on their ongoing life's journey.

The latter is rare; bitter separations are far more common, and where there are children, they suffer greatly. The unresolved conflict between their estranged parents becomes, in turn, a major interruption to their emergence. Take the case of the mother whose son continued to live with his father following a difficult divorce, who felt shocked when five years later her son declared: "Mum, I'm only now getting used to not having you around." It is likely that the boy's statement was an understatement of his experience, but it did prove to be a beginning in building bridges again between himself and his mother.

The Power Of Attraction

What is it that leads us to be attracted to Another, and to a particular Other out of all the many people we meet? There are so many threads to attraction that it can seem mysterious, inexplicable, but attraction is always meaningful, albeit if often at an unconscious level. It is helpful to distinguish between conscious and unconscious attraction. We always know – even when it seems we don't know – what we are looking for! With unconscious attraction, the hidden thing we are often looking for is opportunities to resolve earlier hurts, pain, loss and suffering. Real attraction emerges to the extent that the hidden agenda comes into consciousness and gets responded to openly, rather than protectively.

When we start out in life, we *know* our power of attraction and are prepared to be attracted to the Others in our world – primarily our mothers and fathers. But that natural, open attraction very quickly becomes overlaid with fear, this fear starting even in the womb. We begin to experience not the Real but the Shadow Mother and Father – the fearful, protective Mother and Father – and we begin to create our own Shadow Self in reaction. The attraction between us and Others now becomes fraught; being between Shadow and Shadow and being infused with doubt, insecurity, uncertainty and confusion. We start to express our attraction towards Others and our need for them to be attracted to us in protective rather than in straightforward ways, and we bring those protective ways with us into our adult relationships.

One very common expression of protective attraction in adulthood is the attraction of opposites: you may find yourself unconsciously attracted to someone who is opposite to you in his or her protective strategies – for example, in your passivity you are attracted to someone who is inclined to be aggressive – or opposite to you in his or her hidden expressions of Self. For example, in your hiding of your intelligence, you are attracted to someone who strongly expresses his or her views, opinions, take on things, or opposite to you in regard to earlier experiences of family. For example, coming from a family where there is little sense of togetherness, you are attracted to someone who is very tied up with his or her family. The power of this attraction of opposites is that it provides the opportunity to bring to consciousness the hidden aspects of Self that both of you are needing to re-find.

Take the example of the person whose main protective response is passivity attracting a potential partner who displays considerable aggression. In an earlier book, *Myself, My Partner,* we wrote that when opposites attract, it is that each needs some of the opposite behaviour displayed by the Other. So the person who is passive, for example, needs some of the forcefulness of the Other, and she or he, in turn, needs some of the appeasing and pleasing actions of the passive partner. Since the time of that earlier book, a breakthrough for us was the realisation that actually the last thing either partner needs to develop is another protective response – aggression for the partner who is passive or passivity for the partner who is aggressive. Such responses would only add further interruptions to a relationship that is already severely interrupted. The power of 'opposites' attracting is that sometimes the threatening behaviour of the Other mirrors the way that unconsciously we are with ourselves.

Suppose you are the person who is passive in the case of the attraction between passive and aggressive individuals. You will have mirrored for you by your partner how secretly you aggressively put yourself down all the time, ignore all your own needs and put great stress and pressure on yourself to stay invisible. On the other hand, your aggressive partner who is attracted to your passivity has mirrored for him or her how powerfully he or she 'passes' himself by all the time, takes no active responsibility for himself or herself, and has buried deeply his or her capacity to take responsibility for Self. These breakthroughs for each partner represent the true magic of 'opposites' attracting. The query then that needs to be pursued for each partner is: how am I covertly doing what my partner regularly displays overtly?

Take another common pattern, where you who are hypersensitive to how others see you are attracted to Another who is insensitive to how he or she is with others. You who are hypersensitive to others' perceptions need to come to consciousness of how you are covertly insensitive towards yourself, while your Other also needs to come into consciousness of his or her failure to pay heed to how he or she is with Self. The genius is in how the hidden protective behaviour supports the overt protective behaviour, and both protective responses are the doorway into what real expression of Self has had to be hidden. Another common thread in the attraction of 'opposites' is that the opposing behaviour is what you most experienced in early-life relationship interruptions and the protectors you created then continue to protect you in the here and now.

The further magic is that in attracting what were earlier interruptions into the here and now relationship, there is the opportunity to come out from hiding and say what has been unsayable and do what has been undoable up to now.

This emergence – this breakthrough – will not happen until there is some safe holding for either or both of you outside the intimate couple relationship. A not infrequent adult-adult relationship interruption is where one partner who is possessive is attracted to another who is elusive. The earlier interruption being replayed in the present is where the partner who is possessive, jealous and controlling had an elusive parent who was rarely there for him or her while the elusive partner had a parent who was possessive and wanted the child to live life for the parent. Both partners are now well experienced in how best to unconsciously protect themselves in this repeated unsafe environment.

If and when safe holding occurs for either of the pair, then, for the partner who is possessive, the breakthrough will be 'I need to be strongly here with myself', and for the partner who is elusive 'I need to stay with myself and find that solid interiority from which I hold strong boundaries and can freely express who I uniquely am'. The recreation by both partners of earlier relationship interruptions, in the most amazing way, provides the opportunity for each to break through to the expression of all that had had to be buried, and that now can be resurrected, step by step.

When the breakthroughs occur and there is conscious attraction, you see the Other in all his or her individual glory, you are drawn to that uniqueness, sacredness, preciousness that is the Other's presence, you are attracted to a living presence rather than a medium for hidden needs in yourself.

What Are Lust And Desire About?

The experiences of lust and desire – expressions of your sexual nature – are often seen as gateways to love; whether or not they can operate in this way, the key question again is whether it is your Real or your Shadow Self who is present in any particular experience of lust or desire. The word 'love' is often used to describe the experience of sexual excitement – lust, desire – particularly among the young; a creative confusion possibly representing an unconscious hope that sexual passion will satisfy the heart's longing for love. When considering what lust and desire might have to do with love, it is useful to investigate the felt experience of each and see how they might differ from one another in the quality of the experience.

When you investigate the felt experience of lust, it emerges that the 'I' present is very much the Shadow Self – most likely for both people involved, the 'lusting' and the 'lusted after'. In lust, there is a quality of being lost to the other person, a quality of obsession, a quality of dependence, a quality of fixation. In the experience of lust, I don't even want to 'know' the other person, the Other is a creation of my fantasy; I don't see the Other as a separate, unique, living presence, he or she is reduced to an object of desire; the Other is primarily a vehicle for the satisfaction of my needs, something to be possessed, made mine. But because lust is often a very strong experience, it can be mistaken as a proper basis for intimate, loving relationship. When a couple relationship is formed from lust, it rarely, if ever, survives; it could survive only if both individuals started to find the safety to come home to themselves, to be present to themselves and, as a result, be able to be present to the Other – where there is less of the Shadow and more of the Real Self present.

When desire is present, the quality of the experience is more of wanting this *particular person.* I am more fully present; I am better able to see the Other as being his or her own person;

able to see him or her as an active agent in their own life; I am drawn to this unique presence; I have a sense of wanting to experience the depth and breadth of the Other. Desire is an expression of a powerful life-force – my sexual nature – that wants to reach out and make contact with a particular person. The desire to make connection with another is itself fraught with threat, but because of its conflation with the narrow behaviours of sex it can also be burdened with all the threats – proscriptions and prescriptions – that so often attend sex behaviours.

When desire raises its luminous head, *who is present* will determine how that essential energy is expressed. If you are operating from the Shadow place, desire can become more like lust, raw need, craving or obsession and, if your desire is unrequited, you may feel depressed, rejected, aggressive, may even self-harm or become suicidal. However, it is not desire that gives rise to these protective responses, but the deeper reality of earlier experiences of unrequited reaching out to parents and other significant adults. If you are conscious of your own worthiness, attractiveness and lovability, then when you experience a passion for another you will be open about this attraction and enjoy the 'yes' or, when the answer is 'no', you will be disappointed but not devastated. Furthermore, your desire will not go underground, as it would necessarily do if you were operating from an unconscious, protective inner space.

While desire can be a powerful doorway to a loving relationship with Another, getting to know the Other fully is what lies beyond that door and is what will determine whether or not what desire has initiated will evolve into fuller intimacy. When love does not develop, desire can still be a very happy experience in itself, to the extent that each person is in a more Real rather than a Shadow place. Sadly, when Shadow is present, all kinds of protective responses can be unconsciously created – jealousy, possessiveness, performance anxiety, comparisons, aggression, acquiescence, not voicing what is uncomfortable, and doubting one's physical attractiveness.

While desire may be a more immediate and perhaps rawer experience than loving – which is a voyage of discovery – nonetheless what underlies desire is the heart's pure hunger to connect with Self, with the Other and, ultimately, with infinite and boundless love.

Chapter Three

Early Interruptions

Early Relationships: The Start Of The Path To Intimacy

The path to adult intimacy starts with our early couple relationships – most crucially with our mothers and fathers. The first couple relationship we experience is with our mothers in the womb and, after birth, with our fathers (or father figures). The nature of these first relationships is of profound significance and colours how we are and how we experience every subsequent relationship, including adult intimate relationships. It is important also to remember that each couple relationship – the one with father or mother, sibling, grandparent, teacher, childminder, spouse, employer, colleague or friend – is different because each person brings to it his or her individuality and also their particular story of interruptions to date.

In their efforts to understand their life-stories, and how they responded to what turned up in those stories, clients often wonder how it is that they are where they are while siblings seem to have fared much better, despite being treated, as they see it, in 'exactly the same way' by their parents. When you recognise and honour the fact that the story of the relationship between you and your mother and you and your father is unique to you, then that gives you the solid basis from which to discover what is uniquely being called for now for your wellbeing in relationship with yourself and with others.

The question arises as to what would be a good start on the path to fulfilling, intimate adult relationships. In our innate wisdom we know the truth of who we are: unique, sacred and precious presences in the world, unconditionally worthy of love, responsiveness and respect. But we can hold with this truth only to the extent that it gets reflected back to us from our first entry into the world. You can stay with the truth of who you are when the significant Others in your life relate to you with:

- Wholehearted welcome into the world
- Delight in you
- Respect, joy for your individuality
- Affirmation
- Marking of your presence
- Made to feel the world is a better place because you are in it
- Allowed your own rhythm, pace
- Fascination for you
- Awe at your particularity
- Warm, loving responsiveness
- Engagement with you
- Being present to you
- Being made to feel you are a source of joy
- Emotional attunement
- Empathy
- Connection

If, to any kind of significant degree, you receive what you know to be worthy of you and what you yearn for, then it becomes safe for you to hold your own space in relationship with others, safe for you to engage with others without fear of being taken over by them, of being overwhelmed, of losing your own individuality. You can afford, in turn, to let others have their own place, their own separateness, their own individuality, and you can engage with them, reach out to them, make the connection with them. The Real you can be present when you are grounded in the truth of who you are.

The Impact Of Early Interruptions

Sadly, we do not often get a good start on the path to intimacy. The most common experience in early life is that of interrupted relationships, where we do not get enough of the unconditional love that we deserve and long for. As a result, fear grows in us, and out of that fear we start to hide ourselves away in relationships with others; the interruptions we experienced from others now continue in the relationship with ourselves, and will continue as a hidden agenda driving all other relationships until brought into conscious awareness. Fear grows when what we experience is:

- Pressure to conform
- Not being heard
- Not being held
- Rejection
- Impatience
- Not being attended to
- Being ignored
- Being overruled

- Being ridiculed
- Not taken into account
- Judgment
- Comparisons
- Not being 'got'/understood
- Made to fit others' needs
- Restrictions
- Being made to feel you're not the 'right' daughter/son
- Crossness
- Criticism
- Intimidation
- Forced to go against your own grain
- Seen as a vehicle for others' needs
- Treated as the scapegoat in the family
- Other siblings shown favour over you

Of course, the nature, frequency, intensity and endurance of interruptions to one's presence will range on a continuum from low to very high: from simple annoyance to harshness, or from hurtful to annihilating. It is not too difficult to identify harsh and violent interruptions to our presence – for example, physical violence, starvation, sexual violation, emotional starvation, intellectual denigration, ostracisation, harsh and continual criticism, obvious favouritism, unfavourable comparisons, suffocation of any expression of individuality.

While many will attest to the serious relationship interruptions posed by the kind of harsh and violent behaviours described above, there is often a reluctance – a creative reluctance – to accept that behaviours such as irritability, impatience, perfectionism, overprotection, lack of interest, dismissiveness, annoyance, unrealistic behavioural and educational expectations, over-cautiousness, dominance and over-control also pose considerable threats to the emergence of Self and lead to relationship interruptions.

For example, many people express surprise when they hear that 'tone of voice' can seriously interrupt the spontaneous expression of Self. But just notice what happens emotionally and physically to a child when she or he is shouted at: you will witness in the child's facial expression and body posture and body movement the shock and the horror that a particular behaviour on her or his part could result in such harsh abandonment. Yet the adults who perpetrate these interruptions will often protectively claim: "I was only doing it for the good of the child."

But it is important not to underestimate the legacy of suffering that comes from interruptions that often pass as normal ways of relating between parents and children. Take the not uncommon scene of the young child in the buggy screaming vociferously for attention to some pain, upset or need, and the angry and harsh response from the parent, who is obviously harassed and stressed, is: "You're a very bold child, a very bold child." Other adults will often reinforce this message: "She's been troublesome from the word go"; "there's no pleasing her"; "her poor mother is to be pitied."

The expression of distress that is right for the child is perceived as 'wrong' by the adults and the question that is raised is: "What's wrong with her?" rather than "What's wrong for her?" The child in this case has learned a very severe lesson: it is dangerous to express your distress, you're bad when you do, you won't be heard, and you will be rejected. The child now has to figure out how to manage, how to survive such a threat, and will create protective strategies, such as aggressive expression, or stubbornness, or passivity, or apathy. This, of necessity, all takes place at an unconscious level – for the parent as well as the child – and no real responsiveness is possible until the hidden issues are brought into the light of consciousness.

In early life, it is frequently the case that the greater interruptions occur with one parent rather than with the other. Not surprisingly, the parent who does most of the parenting of children potentially has the greatest impact – for good or ill – depending on whether he or she is operating from an inner solidity or from an inner fearful and protective place. The nature of the impact of the less present parent is also, of course, dependent on the nature of the inner world of that parent. The parent who is not around much but who is openly loving when present can be a wonderful source of security. On the other hand, if the less present parent is in a protective place and is, for example, over-demanding, then that parent, while not around much, is a serious source of interruption.

As children, whether we are sons or daughters, we want so much to be held by a mother and by a father; in order to be free to experience the world, we need to feel safe to express our individual nature both when with male and female Others. When the first female in your life – usually mother – is not able to hold you unconditionally, then, sensibly, you hide away your true self in favour of your mother's protectors because, without some connection with her, you are in serious peril.

Similarly, when the first man in your life – usually your father – does not respond to your unique presence with unconditional warmth, interest, cherishing and affection, you will necessarily repress what is dangerous to express in favour of your father's protective behaviours, because if you do not manage to get him on your side in some way or other, you exist in a perilous limbo. How frightening the world becomes when the most important female and male in your life are sources of threat to your authentic self-expression, and how could you possibly trust either man or woman when you interact with people other than your parents?

In order to stay expressive of one's true Self, as children we require predictable and consistent unconditional holding from each of our parents. A mother providing unconditional love does not compensate for the father who is absent or emotionless or aggressive or passive, and the same applies to the father. It can happen that an individual feels comfortable when with women but loses all sense of Self when with men, this reflecting a 'good enough' relationship with mother and a poor, weak or actively violating relationship with father.

As children, we also need other significant adults in our lives – most especially grandparents, childminders and teachers – to provide the secure holding of unconditional love. As a result of experiences in early holding worlds, many adults lose their inner ground when encountering an authority figure, such as a teacher, doctor, manager or priest. If that adult is a parent, it can be even more challenging for him or her to champion a child of theirs encountering interruptions from one or other of these authority figures, and so the interruptions continue. Parents who are secure within themselves will confidently confront any person whose protective responses darken their child's, or indeed their own, presence. Parents who struggle with acceptance of Self often fail to champion their children's sacredness; somehow, they have not had the opportunities to resolve the non-expression of Self originating in their childhoods.

What is clear is that when any of the significant adults in a child's earlier life act in ways that create fear, even though they may have the best intentions to love, cherish, nurture and empower the child, their unconscious protective state will create interruptions to the adult-child relationship. In their fear-creating responses there is no consciousness that they are re-enacting the very interruptions they, when children themselves, endured and for which they have not yet found the safe emotional holding that would enable them to come out from hiding. It is a case where those unconsciously blind to themselves are also blind to their children's individuality.

Whatever the source of the interruption to expression of our fullness that we encounter as children, it takes a long, long time before we can come to a realisation that the adults who posed threats to our presence were operating from behind the walls of protectors they created as children themselves, in order to survive. There is intelligence to the existence of a long time span before this realisation occurs because trust develops slowly when you have experienced abandonment by the most important individuals in your life. It is only when you can give voice to all the hurts experienced from parents and other significant adults, and you can trust that you can stay true to yourself and live out from your interiority, that you are now in a conscious place to understand and have compassion for the suffering of Others, stay separate from it, and find your own loving care of yourself.

Early Strategies For Surviving Interruptions

By the time any of us come into our adult years, we will have encountered several significant individuals whose sense of Self, and whose behaviour, will to one degree or another have threatened our own habitation of and expression of our individuality. None of these interruptions are intentionally abandoning of our presence but, nonetheless, abandonment is the reality of what happens. This is particularly so for us as infants and children when we are utterly dependent on the adults who have a responsibility of care to us and whom we need to mirror our wondrous presence – the mirroring that enables us to continue to express the fullness of our nature. Those individuals who posed dangers to our self-expression did so from their own unconscious defensiveness in the face of the threats they encountered in the years leading up to adulthood.

When you are in your adult years, the perils of being authentic still exist, but the difference from childhood is that you need no longer be dependent for your survival on parents and other significant adults. As an adult, you can take responsibility for yourself, but this is easier said than done because the protective responses each of us created in childhood were created at an unconscious level.

When we experience interruptions, such as those described above, in our early relationships, in our loving wisdom we find ways of surviving the pain of the interruptions, we find ways of withstanding the protective reactions of those who are central in our lives. We develop our own unconscious protectors and substitute ways of gaining at least some semblance of the love, recognition and visibility we crave and of which we are deprived. We become:

- Timid
- Apathetic
- Wary
- Overly cautious

- Domineering

- Rudderless

- Wanting always to be in the right

- Reserved

- Uncommunicative

- Aggressive

- Controlling

- Passive

- Rebellious

- Terrified of mistakes

- Shy

- Hard

- Overly pleasing

- Focused on success

- Intolerant

- Inconsiderate

- Focused on getting approval

The creation in childhood of our protective strategies signifies the interruption in our own relationship with ourselves that is the inevitable outcome of the interruptions we are experiencing in the relationships with the significant adults in our lives. The depth and breadth of this early interruption in our relationship with ourselves is the critical influence on our openness to the possibility of intimate relationship with Another in adulthood.

The Power Of Our Protective Strategies

While it is true that our protective strategies signify interruptions in our own relationship with Self, there is a power in such interruptions. There is always 'method in our madness' and our protective strategies are wise and creative and serve a very powerful and loving function:

- To eliminate or reduce the experience of current pain arising from threat; to enable us to survive

- To draw attention to the existence of pain

- To anticipate further threats

- To create a substitute means of receiving love and attention

- To alert to past and present interruptions to the emergence of Self

- To keep the issue alive until there is sufficient safety to respond consciously and openly

Our protective strategies are born out of fear. Fear is our first creative emotional response when we encounter an interruption to the expression of our true nature. Fear is wise, being an emergency emotion that alerts you to the need for an emergence, a motion, a movement towards the expression of what is too risky to manifest – for example, your daring, spontaneity, lovability, creativity, and power beyond measure. There is an oft-quoted saying from Marianne Williamson[5] that "our deepest fear is that we are powerful beyond measure" but we believe that there is an even deeper fear and that is the fear of showing our unconditional lovability. The wisdom of this

---

[5] Williamson, Marianne. *Return to Love.* HarperCollins, UK, 1992

deep fear is not about alerting us to the devastating protective responses of the Other, but rather is about the repression, the hiding away and the non-expression of our true and sacred Self that is in danger of happening in the face of the Other's protective responses.

Of necessity, when we are children we create our own protective responses that help us to survive in the face of the protective responses of the significant Others in our lives, but the underlying fear of the tragedy of hiddenness continues, so that the issue is kept alive until the time comes in adulthood when there is sufficient safe holding for us to bring into the light what has had to be hidden of our unique, sacred and precious Selves. This fear is the energy that powers the movement from the necessary hiddenness of childhood to the fullness and openness that becomes possible with safe holding in adulthood – safe holding initially from Others and, ultimately, from oneself.

As children, when we encounter protective behaviours from significant Others, in our wisdom we take care of ourselves in whatever ways we can. Because we cannot face directly the pain of loss of unconditional love, we cannot respond directly to the pain and so have to develop unconscious protective strategies that will at least enable us to have some semblance of love in our lives and thus enable us to survive.

Emotional attunement is essential in our early relationships with mothers and fathers. As infants, we can determine within seconds whether or not the parent is emotionally present, and when such attunement is absent we mask our inherent lovability and stop openly reaching out. The infant may stop making eye contact, physically and emotionally withdraw, or grow aggressive and demanding, or become physically ill. When a child screams for attention, then, at least, the protective response gains some attention, even if only substitute attention. The creation of substitutes ensures survival until the time comes when we experience emotional attunement from Another and can again tentatively explore the possibility of real expression.

Take the case of the child whose mother had not bonded with him owing to her own earlier experiences of abandonment and who had come to realise her fear of reaching out – even to her own child – for fear of re-experiencing the pain of rejection. Her son had begun to sense some change in her, and when they would sit together on the couch watching television, he began to tentatively nudge her, first with his foot – putting his toe in the water of reaching out for love again, so to speak. Previously, he would have kept a safe physical distance from her. His mother noticed his effort to connect and happily was in a place to respond warmly.

Jung[6] was one of the first in a long line of psychoanalysts and psychotherapists to highlight the human truth that unconditional love corresponds to the deepest longing, not only of every child but of every adult. If as a child you encounter an interruption to this fundamental longing, you cleverly hide the precious pearl of your unique presence, and find substitute and protective ways of getting recognition – ways that ingeniously reflect the particular nature of the interruption experienced. For example, if it has been made unsafe for you to express your needs openly – your spontaneous attempts to do so being judged as demanding or selfish or wrong, or your requests being ignored or rejected or punished – then you may find yourself trying to get your needs met in your adult

---

[6] Jung, C.G. *The Essential Jung* (A. Storr, Ed.). Fontana Press, 1983

relationships through being judgmental, critical, demanding of the Other and being rejecting if he or she does not respond in exactly the way you want.

How many times have you heard some person being described as 'totally walled off' or 'impenetrable' or 'absent' or 'just not there' or 'highly defensive' or 'invisible' or 'heartless' or 'impossible to get through to'? One thing you can be absolutely sure of is that the person so described has suffered and is suffering intensely, and that she or he has a story of multiple interruptions to the expression of her or his sacred presence in this world. Any judging, labelling or medicating of these protectors simply adds to the ocean of violations the person has experienced.

You are also likely to have heard individuals described as 'unsure of themselves', 'tentative', 'passive', 'abrasive', 'hostile', 'anxious', 'pushy', 'in your face', 'aggressive', 'passive', 'show-offs', 'shy', 'quiet'. Again, such terms are surface descriptions of hidden suffering, and only the individuals so described can tell the story of the interruptions experienced. It misses the point if we see the person as 'having a problem' or 'having a condition'; it is equally unwise to assume that we know what is going on for them.

It can come as a surprise to realise that passivity is a serious relationship interruption in much the same way as is aggression. How does passivity pose such a threat? Passivity means that the Other – for example, child, partner, friend – in the relationship with you never gets to know you for your true Self because you hide or bury your individuality, what you really feel and what are your legitimate needs. Relationship involves knowing yourself, knowing the Other and ensuring that the Other knows you. Passivity means that you fall at the first hurdle – know yourself – and also means that you fall at the next two hurdles because you are too fearful to get to know the Other and to allow the Other to know you. Fear of rejection dominates your living and keeps you effectively hidden so that the risk of further relationship interruptions from Others is reduced.

Anxiety, too, interrupts relationship. Anxiety means I dare not take risks and I avoid so many adventures. If I am an anxious parent, I will overprotect my children and unconsciously rob them of their natural fearlessness and sense of adventure. Teachers who are anxious about how others see them and anxious about failure will, unwittingly, instil fear in students, such that they, in turn, will begin to bury their natural curiosity and love of learning, or they will try so hard to meet the teacher's unrealistic projections. The wife who is anxious about eating the 'wrong' foods, or the husband who is anxious around socialising, will cause interruptions to the deepening of the intimacy between them.

Of course, the threats to our wellbeing continue beyond childhood and actually multiply in the teenage and adult years as we move into holding worlds beyond the family, and we wisely continue to bring our early protective strategies to bear on these threatening situations. Your protectors were unconsciously devised and you will hold on to them as long as you need them, and you will need them until you find the emotional safety of unconditional love for consciousness to begin to arise about the threats and pain experienced and how you responded to those threats and pain. Our experience is that the individual, whether child or adult, who encounters predictable and consistent emotional holding that is unconditional and empowering will gradually, if tentatively, come out from behind the protective walls and be able to find open, loving care of themselves and be able then to bring the light of their presence to Others.

Leonard Cohen,[7] singer, songwriter and poet, penned the wonderful line "The beauty of our weapons." Each protector is a work of art, a uniquely created response to threats to your presence or to any of the expressions of your wondrous Self. If we see our protectors in any other way, this in turn is a protective reaction which can lead to the endless repetition of the situation whereby protector meets protector, the unlived life meets the unlived life, hidden radiance meets hidden radiance, mask meets mask and fearfulness meets fearfulness.

Taking some of the more common protectors, we illustrate below their creative and substitute purpose.

Protector	**Possible Creative Purpose**
Fearfulness *Substitute function*: you get treated as the 'fragile one'	Hides the fearlessness that has proven dangerous to show and reveals how threatening relationships have been.
Depression *Substitute function:* you get treated as the 'deep one' or the 'troubled one' who needs lots of care	Hides expression of aspects of your true nature that have proved to be 'unsayable' or 'undoable' and reflects all the 'put downs' experienced.
Aggression *Substitute function:* you get seen as the rebel or upstart	Hides hurts experienced and draws attention to those hidden hurts in the hurtful behaviour towards others.
Passivity *Substitute function:* you get seen as the quiet one, or the pleasing one, or the good one	Hides the birthright to live your own life and brings attention to this sad plight by your being there for others but not for yourself.

---

[7] Cohen, Leonard. *First We Take Manhattan.* Sony Music Entertainment Inc.

Self-criticism *Substitute function:* you get seen as the martyr	Hides all that is good about your true nature and reveals the criticisms experienced.
Perfectionism *Substitute function:* you get seen as the perfectionist	You put extreme pressure on yourself to get everything right and at the same time expose all the 'wrongs' encountered.
Compulsively cares for *others, no care for Self* *Substitute function:* you get seen as the carer	You poignantly show how dangerous it was made for you to be there for yourself.
Helplessness and high *dependence* *Substitute function:* you get seen as the helpless one	You can do little or nothing for yourself; hiding your power beyond measure and revealing how threatening it would be for you to show your power.

These different scenarios give you some idea of the complexity of human processes and demonstrate that unless there is a rise in consciousness, these ways of surviving will repeat themselves in subsequent relationships. Taking the above protective behaviours as examples, a potential partner will encounter the following from the individual manifesting the particular protector:

- "Take care of me"

- "Don't get too close"

- "Don't upset me"

- "Let me please you"

- "I will never be good enough for you"

- "I need everything to be perfect"

- "I will do everything for you"

- "I depend on you to look after me"

When you are consciously living from the inside out, your responses to individuals who have to live their lives from the outside in will be one of non-judgment and compassion. But you will never allow your own precious life to be compromised by the unlived life of the Other. You will certainly support the Other in becoming more conscious and more independent and separate. When such mature responses on your part fall on unconsciously deaf ears, then, for both your sakes, you will gently close the door on the relationship. When you conform to or collude with the hidden projections of the Other, then, inevitably, the relationship will go into crisis, not only because of the presence of the interruptions of the projections and introjections but also because a deeper call is being made – the call for each of you to come home to yourself, as this is the only way you can effectively create a home with the Other.

Chapter Four

Did I Get To Meet Myself Before I Met You?

Your Relationship with Yourself: The Crucial Issue

When it comes to you meeting a potential intimate partner, the crucial influence on what transpires between you is the nature of the inner relationship each of you has with yourselves. As you have seen, how you are with yourself in adulthood is the outcome of the nature of the relationships you experienced with significant Others in your early life. If you have experienced few, and not very serious, interruptions in early relationships, you will have had the safety to develop an openly loving relationship towards yourself.

But if interruptions have been anything more than minor, then you protectively will have hidden away aspects of yourself; you protectively will have developed a Screen Self; you protectively will have disconnected from your worthiness of love – you will have an interrupted relationship with yourself. There will now be a hidden agenda driving the relationship with the Other; this agenda revolves around earlier losses, hurts and suffering which you covertly hope the Other will resolve for you.

In the thrill and excitement of first meeting someone, there is often the hope that the longed-for unconditional love will finally happen, and that it will now be possible to reveal your true Self and no longer have to hide away aspects of your unique presence. But that hope can be quickly shattered when you begin to encounter strong protective responses in your loved one. When you are in a hidden place yourself – when your Screen Self is present – you will find yourself countering the Other's protective behaviour with protectiveness of your own. If you happen to be occupying your own individuality and have established your own inner solidity and independence – in other words, when your Real Self is present – you will spontaneously and compassionately challenge the Other's threatening behaviour, as much for the Other's sake as for your own.

Sadly, few of us come into our adult years without having suffered blows to some aspects of our presence – physical, sexual, emotional, intellectual, behavioural, social or creative – and so more commonly it is a case of Screen meeting Screen. While necessary and purposeful, every protector we create becomes a potential offence to another's presence. Underlying this is the unconscious hope that the person who is hurt by your protective actions will see the hidden unresolved hurts that you are also carrying – will see behind the Screen. This process is much the same as when you 'behave badly' as a child – such as having a temper tantrum – and your hope is that your parent will understand that this behaviour reflects some hurt, distress, or pain that you cannot openly name; you are hoping that your parent will break through to what lies hidden. You are longing for understanding, compassion, empathy, loving responsiveness, all of which you are worthy of but you have become too fearful to seek openly.

Any one of us who is hidden and has masked our fears wants desperately to be loved. But we dare not risk expression of this fundamental human need when parents, and other significant adults did not provide the unconditional love that is critical for us as children. If our parents could not be trusted, how can we now trust anybody else – certainly not a newfound potential partner?

Ultimately, the resolution lies in trusting ourselves, but there can be a lot of path to travel before we find the safety to reach that destination. If, for example, my father – the king of my childhood world – found me to be not the 'right' daughter for him, how am I going to risk showing myself to this new person? The terror of recurrence of such pain will be too much for me until I begin to find some connection with the felt experience of that first severely interrupted relationship. Connecting with that felt experience can be hugely painful and I will need strong, persistent safe holding in order to face into it, and begin to find loving responsiveness to myself now, and understanding that I never deserved that from my father and that his response to me was reflective of his own dark inner world and had nothing whatsoever to do with me. This is not an easy path to travel but this is the path to real intimacy. If my story remains in the unconscious, then unwittingly I will bring all that hidden suffering, and my protective responses to that suffering, to bear on my relationship with the Other.

The ideal would be that you would have been in the habit of reflecting on how you are with yourself before attraction to another occurs. Reflection can be painful, and you may cleverly put it on the long finger, but non-reflection is far more painful because you remain stuck in an ever-deepening burial of your real self. As you have seen, the nature of the relationships in childhood is what led to the necessary interring of your real Self and the repression of many – or all – aspects of your individual presence. If, in your early adulthood, you feel at one with yourself, you will wish to bring that fullness to another and experience, in turn, his or her fullness. This is the openly loving relationship with Another to which we all aspire.

But if you feel empty inside – the depth of the void leading to different degrees of internment of Self – then that emergency inner state will reveal itself internally and externally on a daily basis. Accordingly, the crucial theme for reflection when you come to meet a partner is how are you with yourself, and to what degree you give expression to the depth and complexity of your individual and unique presence – to what degree are you present to yourself and present to the Other?

Degrees Of Being Present: To Yourself, To The Other

Broadly speaking, we can distinguish three levels of being present: fully present, partially present and absent, these being expressed in different kinds of outward behaviour as described below. In reflecting on the degree to which you are present in any particular relationship, it is important to realise that others will have their own perceptions of your behaviour and level of presence, and how others see you will often not be how you see yourself. But you are the expert – and the only expert – in this regard. Others may adopt the protective stance of believing that they can identify and describe the truth of who you are but, of course, this is something they cannot do. Nobody has access to your inner world, that is your private sanctum. Furthermore, how others perceive you and respond to your protectiveness will reflect their own level of protectiveness.

The person whose real Self is present will seek to gain an understanding from you, to get underneath your protective behaviour so that she or he may gain the prize of getting to know the real you. You may find yourself quite shocked when openly and lovingly confronted with how your protective behaviour poses a threat to others but, of course, that shock is not surprising in light of the reality that our protectors are unconsciously created. The fact that you allow yourself to feel shocked is the beginning of consciousness of your protective behaviours; consciousness of their source, creative and loving purpose, and consciousness of the opportunity now present to bring forward what has long lain hidden behind the protectors.

Bringing into conscious awareness your inner sense of yourself and your outward stance towards others can be a major challenge. The profiles below are an attempt to make what can be a complex reflection more manageable, but it is important that they do not mask the fact that no two people's repertoire of behaviours are ever completely the same. Individuals who are more fully present will feel good about themselves: they will feel confident, peaceful and calm within, they will feel unconditional love and compassion for themselves and for others, and they will be authentic, real, just and fair in their dealings with others. Such people are also often spiritual in their outlook on life.

Individuals who are partially present but protectively narcissistic, in an unconscious bid to survive all the 'let downs' they have experienced to date on their path, may feel themselves as being hard done by, distrustful of others' motivations, have a punishing attitude to people who do not meet their needs, an over-drive to succeed, often at the expense of the wellbeing of others. Even though such people may frequently feel fearful, they will not admit this to anybody but will creatively put on a brave and tough face to mask what they really feel.

Individuals who are partially present but protectively passive and over-pleasing will be convinced that their purpose in life is to care for others, not rock the boat, not upset people, and be considerate only of others' needs and never of their own. They can suffer from overwhelming guilt when they do not meet another's needs. They will bend over backwards for others, and they can frequently feel exhausted from the relentless caring for others. The motives for the apparently selfless behaviour lie in the unconscious and are concerned with having an identity that is tied to needing others – to need others so that they can feel some connection to others; some contact, even if conditional, being better than no contact. There exists an emotional void within, a hunger for love, but this realisation will remain below the surface until the day comes when they encounter an unconditional relationship where they are consistently loved for themselves.

People who might be described as absent feel they are nothing and that nobody could possibly love them. They can be dangerously aggressive towards others or completely withdrawn – physically, emotionally, sexually, and socially – from others. They may believe that they are bad and that nobody would want to have anything to do with them. Their thoughts can be of a highly aggressive nature, where they believe that others are out to get them; or they can turn the anger on themselves and be devastatingly self-critical – out to get themselves before others get there before them. They are often addicted to substances – food, alcohol, prescribed drugs, illegal drugs – and can have a range of process addictions, also ways of filling the void within, for example, animal rights, political revolution, work, the hoarding of useless objects, an all-consuming hobby, sports, or fitness.

Those individuals who in adulthood have the inner safety to be present to themselves and to others are those fortunate enough to have had early relationships that have been largely of an unconditionally empowering nature. Their parents, and other significant adults in their holding worlds, would have inhabited their own individuality and, consequently, have been in a place not to interrupt the emergence of the real Self in their young charges. It is a tragic reality that only a small percentage of adults operate from that solid interiority, and the adults who have experienced interruptions themselves – unless resolved – become the source of interruptions to their children's natural expression of Self. This cycle of interruptions leading to more interruptions can be broken only when at least one of the parties in the relationship finds the safety to resurrect his or her expression of Self.

Current Interruptions In Your Relationship With Yourself

When two people first meet, the temptation often is – a temptation strongly reinforced by family, friends and society – to assess the potential of the relationship by focusing on the Other, and on his or her exterior characteristics. If, for example, he or she ticks the boxes of 'good looking', steady job, right age, no obvious 'flaws', the sex is good, then we may feel that that is a sound basis for entering into an intimate relationship. But we are looking protectively the wrong way, the real test of the potential of the relationship being the extent to which each of the two individuals involved has come into an openly loving relationship with themselves – or at least has the willingness to embark on that path. You are the expert on the nature of your relationship with yourself and, conversely, you have no expertise on how the Other is with him or herself – only the Other really knows the nature of that relationship.

The essential question then for each person to ask consciously is: "Who in the here and now am I bringing to the person with whom I'm wanting a relationship?" "How do I see myself and, from that interior relationship with myself, how do I relate to the Other?" The operative word here is *consciously*. You may find yourself, like most people, tending not to reflect on your interior world, your focus being more on the other person. But, as Aristotle said: "A life unexamined is a life not lived" – his words emerging from his mentor Socrates, who advocated "Know yourself." When conscious examination of one's inner world does not take place, it is inevitable that interruptions will arise in the relationship between the two people because the relationship is protective rather than real in nature, surviving rather than thriving. In the protective relationship, each person masks fears, doubts and insecurities, and hopes that the Other will resolve these hidden issues, thereby avoiding the risk of authentic expression.

The reality is that it is only *you* who can begin to relate from within; wanting the Other to do it is passing the responsibility for your precious life on to another, and no matter how hard the other person tries, it is never going to be good enough – indeed, it is a bottomless pit. When both of you in the relationship are looking to each other to fill the emptiness within, then the relationship between you will gradually crumble under the weight of an impossible responsibility. When each of you finds the emotional safety to examine your own interiority and begins to travel the long and painful but exciting journey inwards, then you can be mutually supportive on that essential journey. The provision of that mutual support powerfully strengthens the couple relationship and provides the safety for the paradoxical basis for fulfilment and real intimacy – separateness and all-one-ness.

Uncovering Current Interruptions In The Relationship With Yourself

A useful way to bring to consciousness the protective strategies you will have developed in response to early relationship interruptions, and that now form your own interrupted relationship with yourself, is to consider the questions set out below. It is an indicator of a shift to consciousness when you are ready to pose a question for yourself; you are on the quest for the emergence of all that you have wisely hidden behind your walls of protectors.

In engaging in this investigation, it is important that you remember that these strategies were created by your loving, wise Self to protect you in times of serious threat (see Chapter Three). Your protectors call not for judgment, or rejection, but rather for understanding of the story behind them, and for compassion, warmth, kindness, empathy for the person who lived through that story.

Physical Interruptions

If there have been, and continue to be, interruptions in your relationship with your physical self, these may find expression in the following protectors:

- Carelessness around physical needs
- Using your body for hidden ends – for example, to seduce another
- A mechanical attitude towards your bodily needs
- Ignorance of how your body works
- Ignoring what your body is telling you
- Hating your body
- Feeling disgust for your body
- Over- or under-eating
- Over- or under-exercising
- Comparing your body with others
- Being punishing of your body
- Being rejecting of your body
- Subjecting your body to harsh treatment
- Addiction to the 'body beautiful'

Sexual Interruptions

Interruptions in your relationship with your sexual self may find expression in the following protectors:

- Confusing sexuality with sex
- Using sex for other agendas, such as to feel powerful
- Being focused on sex performance
- Crudeness in describing sexual behaviour or bodily parts
- Feeling shame around sexuality and sexual desires
- Being sexually promiscuous in behaviour
- A sense of deadness

- Being obsessed with sexual matters
- Avoiding anything to do with sexuality
- Being addicted to sex

Emotional Interruptions

Interruptions in your relationship with your emotional self may find expression in the following protectors:

- Ignoring feelings
- Dismissing feelings
- Ridiculing feelings
- Repressing feelings
- Fighting against feelings
- Struggling with having feelings
- Being bland
- Maintaining an 'even keel' at all times
- Being frightened of feelings
- Being hysterical

Intellectual Interruptions

Interruptions in your relationship with your intellectual self may get expressed in the following protectors:

- Diminishing your intelligence
- Ignoring your intelligence
- Hiding your intelligence
- Pursuing success
- Labelling – for example, stupid, brainy, slow, average, university material

- Avoiding mistakes
- Deferring to others' views, perceptions
- Seeing others always as the real experts

Behavioural Interruptions

Interruptions in your relationship with your behavioural self may get expressed in the following protectors:

- Forever analysing
- Judging
- Being overly cautious
- Being continuously wary
- Acting helpless
- Acting the victim
- Being passive
- Staying stuck
- Being dependent on others
- Intruding in the Other's space
- Being controlling

Social Interruptions

Interruptions in your relationship with your social self may get expressed in the following protectors:

- Being conformist
- Staying hidden
- Being retiring
- Being pushy
- Being shy

◗ Being overwhelming

◗ Being anxious

◗ Being invisible

Creative Interruptions

Interruptions in the relationship with your creative self may get expressed in the following protectors:

◗ Staying with proscriptions and prescriptions

◗ Acting as restricted

◗ Acting as burdened

◗ Being pessimistic

◗ Being fearful of risk

◗ Holding back

◗ Sticking to the 'known'

The power of bringing into consciousness the protectors you may have wisely and lovingly created, in regard to different expressions of your Self, is that they are the window into what has been missing for you in your relationship with yourself, and that conscious knowledge enables you to fill the void, to respond openly to unfulfilled yearnings for what you are worthy of and deserve. An open, loving relationship with yourself, and the many ways in which that gets expressed inwardly and outwardly, is the subject of later chapters.

Chapter Five

Did I Know What I Was Looking For?

Seeking A Partner From Old Interruptions

In the search for your intimate partner, it is crucial to recognise that you bring with you whatever interruptions in your relationship with yourself (see the previous chapter) have developed, and that those interruptions will manifest in hidden agendas that you will bring to the Other. Becoming more consciously aware of those hidden agendas, and the underlying hitherto unsayable truths about your real Self that are seeking to break through, gives you a head-start on the path to finding a real, intimate relationship with Another. The understanding of your own story enables you to shift from being 'stuck' in the past to movement, to aliveness, to connection in the here and now.

Most couple relationships are formed from unconscious longings and hopes, and the desire to resolve old hurts and losses; the seeking of intimacy coming from the void rather than from fullness. The paradox is that, on the one hand, we apparently do not know what we are getting ourselves into when we first meet, but in fact we do know – at an unconscious level. There is always a meaning and purpose to the attraction but this may have to be kept hidden below consciousness. For example, if you consciously knew that your attraction to the Other was because he or she is like a parent – mother or father – with whom you have experienced many unresolved interruptions, would you be likely to plunge yourself into such a relationship? Hardly! But this is precisely what you need to do ultimately to find your freedom, independence and self-reliance.

The power of the attraction is that it creates a second and major opportunity for you to find your own place in the relationship with Another; to be able to be your own person, to stand separate in your own space, secure in your worthiness of love and the preciousness and sacredness of your unique presence. Out of that separateness you can make free and open connection with the Other – no struggle with the Other, no trying to fit around him or her, no having to survive the Other's protective behaviours as you necessarily and wisely did with your parents. But the 'knowing' of the individual, who through his or her protectors will provide the powerful opportunities for you to become conscious of your precious presence, needs to be unconscious, for who of us would be ready once again to consciously face into the possibility of recurrence of interrupted experiences?

In the seeking of Another which is coming from a history of interrupted relationships, you have the wise but hidden purpose of:

- ◗ Re-creating the threatening dynamics of earlier interrupted relationships

- ◗ Creating the opportunities for freeing yourself of the imprisonment of yourself that had to occur in response to earlier relationship interruptions

» Bringing into the open the unsayables and
   undoables rooted in earlier relationships

» Providing the necessary opportunities for you
   to come home to your real, authentic Self

When you seek an intimate Other from a history of
interrupted relationships – including a current interrupted
relationship with yourself – as all of us do to one degree or
another, then there will always be a hidden agenda in the
search. At one level – in your core, in your innate wisdom
– you know that what you seek, and long for, and deserve
is an open, unconditionally loving relationship. But when
your original reaching out for such open loving has been
met with conditionality – you must look and act in certain
ways to attract love – then you become wary of openly
and straightforwardly expressing your desire for loving
connection. The underlying sense is 'I want it, but I don't
want to show my hand in case you'll reject me and I could
not bear to re-experience the pain of rejection. So I'm hoping
that you will spot my lovability, that you will be drawn to me
without my having to take the risk of coming into the open'.

Arising from interrupted relationships in childhood, the
deepest fear is of openly expressing the truth of who you
actually know yourself to be: a unique, sacred and precious
presence in the world, unconditionally worthy of love.
Finding Another to declare that truth for us is our proximate
protective goal, but the ultimate real goal is to find the inner
safety that will enable us to declare, and act from, that truth
ourselves. This is the finding of the inner stronghold that John
O'Donohue[8] so accurately and beautifully describes: the inner

---

[8] O'Donohue, John. *Anam Chara*. London: Bantam Press, 1997

stronghold of love from which nobody can ever again reject, demean, abandon or devastate you – this is the resolution of the interrupted relationship with yourself. The strange thing is that it is the relationship with another human being, and all their accompanying story, suffering and protectors, that provides the most powerful waymarkers to that inner stronghold. But we need to consciously realise that this is so, and consciously work with the opportunities thrown up for us by the interruptions that automatically arise when two people come together in an intimate relationship.

The route to the inner stronghold of unconditional love is conscious, compassionate awareness of your story and the consequent protectors that you have developed, the ways that you have kept yourself protectively hidden, the expressions of yourself that you have suppressed, and the meeting with Another on their own particular route brings the opportunities for the emergence of that conscious awareness. So, we always know what we are about, what we need and deserve, but it is the nature of the human condition that we have to go about it in a roundabout, unconscious way because of the fear – the terror – arising from interruptions in our early relationships.

Current interruptions give us the opportunity to make a connection with the felt experience of earlier interruptions and, in making that connection, find loving responsiveness for ourselves now. Of course, our parents, and other significant adults in our childhoods, would never have wanted to oust us from that natural inner stronghold of unconditional love, but because they had been ousted from it themselves, they inevitably led us far, far away from our real, loving home. But, as you have seen, we are not at the mercy of our stories, we have always lovingly created our strategies for survival and, as adults, we have the chance that we did not have as children to use our wise, loving creativity now for living, for expressing the fullness of who we are, for wholeness.

Uncovering The Hidden Agenda

The real power of intimate relationship with another – the possibility of returning to your inner stronghold of unconditional love – can be released to the extent that the hidden projective agendas at play for each partner are brought into conscious awareness. While the hidden agendas stay hidden, interruptions inevitably occur and continue; wisely so, because interruptions are the alarm bell alerting you to the fact that there are hidden needs seeking to be brought into the light. At a level deeper than hidden needs are truths about your presence that have been too dangerous to reveal; for example "I am a unique, precious and sacred presence in the world, always worthy of unconditional love. Love is my essence and my driving force."

In the here and now of your intimate relationship, the important question is: what are you looking for from your intimate Other, and what do you think the Other is looking for from you? Clearly, the other person in the relationship with you needs to be asking the same question. The answers may not have been revealed but are seeking to come into the open; the fundamental truth being whether or not you are seeing your Other through a protective lens – either projection of your needs on to the Other or introjection of the Other's needs – or with real eyes. If you are relating from an inner solidity, you will see the Other for the sacred and precious presence that he or she truly is.

Furthermore, you will want the Other to know you for the sacred and precious presence that you are. You will be curious to know how the Other sees himself or herself because only he or she knows who they really are. There is excitement in the discovery of the Other's individuality through their revelation of their Self to you. In your openness to the Other, you are a true and powerful guardian of your own and the Other's individuality, of the fundamental all-one-ness of both of you and of your mutual birthright to consciously live and take responsibility for your one wild and precious life.

What a blessing you bring to the Other when you see him or her in this way. Sadly, such openness is not common; the more usual situation is that we protectively look to the Other for what we need to be looking for from ourselves. We are blinded to the Other because of our hidden agenda of wanting some proof from the Other of our lovability, of wanting the Other to mind and take care of us, to take responsibility for how our lives work out. Some examples of how you may project responsibility for your life on to Another and the hidden agenda at play are:

 ▻ "You must live your life for me (so I'll feel secure in the world)"

 ▻ "I'll live my life for you (so you'll never leave me and I'll know that I'm lovable and worth something)"

 ▻ "You're never there for me (so I get the message across that I'm terrified of abandonment)"

 ▻ "I can't ever be there for you (so I won't have to have the terror of failing you)"

You Must Live Your Life For Me!

When you protectively view your Other as being responsible for your life and wellbeing, and the Other in turn protectively takes on this role, you may describe the Other as kind, caring, selfless, generous, sensitive, obliging and thoughtful and, overall, wonderful to you, these being qualities that are very likely to be absent from the relationship with yourself. In unconsciously wanting your Other to live life for you, you are revealing your insecurity about having persistent, secure, loving care, and you are wanting the Other to be the kind of parent you would wish to have had, but tragically did not have.

In your insecurity, any hint of your Other needing space and time for Self can release a backlash on your part as your terror of a repetition of earlier lack of care raises its painful head. The hidden intention of any aggressive, dominating, manipulative or controlling responses is to get the Other back on the track of living life for you. If earlier experiences of neglect were frequent, intense and enduring over time, you may find yourself being very possessive of the Other, jealous and even paranoid that he or she is having an affair or is planning to leave the relationship.

Inevitably, the interruption escalates as your Other cannot possibly fill the bottomless pit of your unrequited longing for secure, loving care – only you can do that – and as adults we need to be giving ourselves that care. But there is a wisdom in selecting the Other whom you unconsciously know is going to try to live life for you, because all of what you are looking for from him or her is what you need to be giving to yourself; you have covertly chosen the perfect partner for what needs to come into consciousness for you. So, of course, has the

Other chosen the perfect partner in you! Consciousness of the projections – and introjections – that are occurring between you will begin only when one or other of you finds some level of safe holding with somebody outside the couple relationship in which to begin the necessary reflection (see Chapter Seven).

The co-dependent nature of this kind of relationship is evident in the fact that neither partner feels that they can stand alone, and each feels that they would fall apart without the Other. Curiously, there is often social reinforcement or praise for this kind of dependent dance: "He's a wonderful husband; he does everything for her." "He's blessed with the wife he has; she's always there for him, always thinking of his needs." "She fell on her feet when she found him; he'd do anything for her." "You're so lucky to have someone who only thinks of you." "It's nice to be looked after." While the hidden agenda of needing some level of security may be met to some extent, and for a period of time, unless the underlying truth – "I'm immensely capable and have everything I need to look after my wellbeing, and my wellbeing deserves to be looked after"– can come into the open, the inner interruption in your own relationship with Self continues, and so too does the likelihood continue of interruptions occurring in the relationship with the Other. So too does the likelihood continue of these interruptions becoming more severe over time. It is the truth that sets us free   free to be ourselves – and that opens up the possibility of real connection, and true intimacy with the Other.

I'll Live My Life For You!

If you find yourself being the one who tries to live your life for the Other, the unconscious hope operating within you is that if you are always there for the Other, then the Other will love you and never leave you. This unconscious drive to live life for the Other can often arise as a creative response to an over-demanding parent, or to a parent who was frequently sick and communicated helplessness. The behaviour of over-pleasing and attempting to do everything for such a parent is the child's attempt to get at least some recognition through being the 'good little child' in a situation where she or he is not cherished for their unique and precious presence. The projection that 'the Other cannot do without me' is the mirror opposite of the projection that 'I cannot do without the Other'. If the partner who is controlling is unwittingly abrogating conscious responsibility for Self, so too the partner who is the 'giver' and who sacrifices his or her life for the Other is abrogating conscious responsibility for his or her own precious life.

The creative strategy here is to make yourself so indispensable to the Other that you have at least the substitute comfort of being needed, rather than having to express the more terrifying need to be loved unconditionally for yourself. Over the years, we have encountered many individuals who have been condemned by a parent, partner, or friend when they attempted to assert "I need to be loved for myself rather than what I do for you." Of course, such condemnation reflects the unlived lives of those who aggressively demean another's bid for freedom. The strategy of "I'll live my life for you", while wise and necessary, works for you only while the Other remains dependent on you; should he or she find their own self-reliance and independence, you will have lost your protective identity. Real resolution happens when it becomes safe for you to openly declare, and act out from, the truth seeking to break through; the truth in this case being: "My presence matters; I make a difference by being here; I deserve to be loved for my presence."

You're Never There For Me; I Can't Ever Be There For You!

If you, or your Other, are operating from the projection of either "you're never there for me" or "I can't ever be there for you", your relationship will be characterised by 'absence' and is likely to be experienced as an emotional desert. In this kind of relationship, many substitutes come into play in an attempt to compensate for the absence of love. Some of the powerful substitutes that may be used include addiction to work, perfectionism, addiction to success, obsession with sex, obsession with pornography, substance addictions – for example, food, alcohol, drugs – fanatical involvement in some particular activity – for example, sports, physical fitness, animal welfare, a political movement, reading, music or the internet. These creative reactions provide some comfort in the absence of emotional holding and would have been devised in earlier years and, unconsciously, brought into the intimate relationship.

The protective strategy of absence in the relationship reflects a story of severe interruptions whereby the person was not allowed to live his or her own separate, individual life. A common earlier interruption is that of a parent acting from the projection of "you're never there for me". The message that gets communicated to the child is: "Your life has meaning only to the extent that you will be there for me, and you'd better be on your toes to measure up to my expectations." This projection comes from huge fear and, in turn, creates huge fear. The person (parent) acting from the protective stance of "you're never there for me" most likely has a story of severe abandonment. The hidden agenda is: "Won't someone please see that I need care and give it to me." The truth seeking to emerge into the open is: "I am the guardian of my own wellbeing and I deserve to have my wellbeing guarded." The child at the receiving end of the projection of "you're never there for me" now experiences the huge fear of failing the Other – the responsibility is too weighty, is impossible to fulfil – and the protective stance likely to be developed by the child is: "I can't ever be there for you." The deeper underlying truth seeking to emerge into the open is: "The only life for which I can carry responsibility is my own; that is the only responsibility that is worthy of me."

The stance of absence from the Other symbolically represents that person's absence from Self, a necessary disconnection from any expression of Self in the face of earlier, terrifying abandonment experiences. This disconnection is an act of love, a safeguarding of the pearl of great price – one's precious presence – and this hidden love will be consciously activated only when the person encounters unconditional holding from Another. Such holding provides the opportunity for the person in adult years who is still imprisoned by childhood abandonments to begin the long trek home to conscious expression of their unique and precious presence.

The Power Of Projections And Introjections

It is amazing to witness how each child in a family creates different survival strategies in the face of interruptions in the relationships with parents and with other significant adults. Interruptions that themselves come out of the tragedy of the adults' own unlived lives.

The particularity of each child's experience becomes very evident in the family reunion; hearing the adult members' reminiscences, you would swear that each came from a different family and had a different mother and father – and the reality is that they did! There is that wonderful dynamic whereby each parent projects something different on to each child – usually there are very different projections on to sons and daughters – and each child, in turn, amazingly manufactures his or her own protectors, either introjections or projections, against what is being projected.

Given the interplay of child-adult unconscious protectors in our early relationships, it is understandable that our relationships as adults are often densely populated by our own and the Other's different kinds of introjections and projections. Some examples are given below to help you reflect on what introjections and projections you may be bringing to your relationship and the interplay of projections and introjections that may be occurring between you both.

Projection	Introjection
"You're my everything"	"I'll devote myself completely to you"
"You make my world go round"	"I'll make my world around you"
"You were made for me"	"I'll give all my attention to you"
"You're my Launcelot"	"I'll be your saviour"
"You can make my dreams come true"	"I'll make your dreams mine"
"You light up my life"	"I'll be the light of your life"
"Only you can make me happy"	"I'll devote my life to making you happy"
"Won't you take care of me?"	"I'm the one to take care of you"
"Won't you always be there for me?"	"I'll let you always be the one to call the shots"
"You are the only one for me"	"I'll make sure I do a good job"

Clearly, our unconsciously formed expectations of ourselves and of the Other place a burden on the relationship and lead to interruptions. But, of course, that is never our intention. Our real desire is to be fully present in the relationship – present to ourselves and present to the Other. It is in being fully present that we find our greatest joy and aliveness in relationship; we know this in our core but fear gets in the way – the very real and terrible fear of being rejected, ignored, dismissed, rubbished, annihilated. Our protectors – projections and introjections – mask what we fear is unsayable and undoable, which is that I deserve to be at the centre of my own life for, indeed, there is no other place I can be; each one of us is a world unto itself, sacred, unique and precious.

In order to release the power of our protective strategies of projection and introjection, we need to bring them back to ourselves; we need to uncover all that we dare not do or say and begin to give expression to the truth of ourselves. Using the examples above, when we perceive the projections and introjections as being important messages about our own relationship with Self, what needs to become conscious is apparent:

▶ "I'm everything to me"; "the most important person to love me is me"; "I'm whole and entire in myself"

▶ "I'm the one who makes my world go round"; "I'm the one in the driving seat in my life"; "I take charge of my life myself"

▶ "I was made for me"; "I was given life for me"; "I dare to be myself, to stay true to myself"; "I stand by the truth of my own separate life"

▶ "I'm my own saviour"; "I'm the one who knows what saving is needed"; "the only life I can save is my own life and I deserve that saving"

▶ "I can make my dreams come true"; "I give weight to my dreams"; "I listen to my own inner voice"; "I stand by what I know in my heart to be true and right for me"

▶ "I need and deserve to be there for myself"; "I need to live my particular life"; "I walk my own journey"; "I am self-reliant and immensely capable"

- ❱ "I need to light up my life with unconditional love for myself"

- ❱ "Happiness is fleeting; I have a deeper vision – the vision of unconditional loving holding of myself at all times"

- ❱ "I deserve care, I have the resources to do it, and I will do it"

- ❱ "I will always be there for myself with understanding, compassion and loving responsiveness"

- ❱ "I am the one for me – that is the ultimate marriage"

Chapter Six

Where Are We Now As A Couple?

The Past Is In The Present

As you have seen, the person to whom you are drawn to begin with is coloured by the story of your early relationships, and your current relationship with yourself. When you have embarked on a relationship with Another, consciousness of the manner in which your individual stories interweave is of crucial importance in facilitating the emergence of true intimacy between you. As long as the interactions between you are governed by unconscious past experience, then interruptions in your relationship with one another will inevitably occur and continue.

It is important to keep bearing in mind that it is the nature, depth and breadth of your relationship with yourself that determines the nature of your relationship with the Other – this, of course, being a two-way street. Your path to conscious wholeness will be peopled by Others who are suffering just as you do, and who are also doing the best they can to avoid or alleviate such suffering. When you become conscious of the true nature of the I-You relationship you can certainly provide unconditional love, understanding, compassion and support, and you can show belief in the power of the Other to fully emerge, but you cannot take on for another the fundamental human task of finding the inner stronghold that provides the safe ground for conscious emergence.

Making Connection With The Felt Experience Of The Child

In becoming conscious of the suffering and protective strategies that you are bringing from your past into your current relationship, making connection with the felt experience of the child you were is hugely powerful. The felt experience is the most important information for your wellbeing. When you are a child, you cannot connect with your felt experience; it would be overwhelming because you are not in a position to hold it and respond to it, so you have to repress it, act in disregard of it, find a way of surviving it. But that disconnection, while necessary, loving and wise in the circumstances, means that your wellbeing also is at one remove. When you are in touch with all the threads of the felt experience, all the sensitivities, all the sore places, then you know precisely what in particular is being called for in your care; you know what choice, decision, action will be the best match for what is happening in your life.

Suppose, for example, that you have grown up with a sense that to be 'good' means to have no needs of your own because to have needs would be judged as putting further pressure on an already hard-pressed parent. As an adult, you find yourself at the mercy of demands from others but you try your best to measure up to the learned ideal of the 'good' person until a crisis – perhaps of health, of burn-out – brings the issue to the forefront. If you find the safety to connect with the felt experience of trying to be the good child who has no needs of your own, you will uncover all the anxiety, sadness, heaviness, fear, confusion, stress, emptiness, unreality that go with that experience.

If you can allow in all that information, if you can listen and hear, then you have the perfect informational base from which to figure out what care you need in the here and now in the face of demands from Others. This care might look like making decisions about what level of responsiveness to the Other sits well with you, feels OK for you, sits lightly with you. The care may involve making choices and decisions about limits, about what needs to happen for your needs to be looked after properly. You will be able to find an answer for your care rather than shooting in the dark. In finding in the here and now the kind of responsiveness to your particular situation that you deserve, and that was not available to you as a child, you clear the space for true intimacy between you and the Other, rather than being stuck in a dependent dance where the hidden agenda is "if I do all this for you, won't you see that I too need that kind of care?"

Querying Where You Are As A Couple

A central conscious question for each person in the couple relationship to ask is: "What aspects of interrupted relationships with parents, or significant others such as grandparents, childminders, teachers, siblings, are seeking to break through for resolution in this present relationship?" What you have hidden about yourself, the creative fears you have developed, the protective strategies you have devised, and earlier unmet needs will all be unconsciously present in the here and now couple relationship. In some amazing way, in the selection of the particular Other, you cleverly reactivate your early unresolved painful experiences with those adults who – sadly for them and for you – were not in a place to provide what Winnicott[9] calls 'the good-enough' emotional holding

[9] Winnicott, D.W. *The Family and Individual Development.*
London: Free Association Press, 1965

required for the true emergence of Self. The hidden purpose is to have a second chance to find your own separate place in an I-Thou relationship where there is a fully present 'I' – safe to take your unique place in the world. In investigating the present nature of your relationship, it can be useful to consider the following questions:

- In what ways is what happened in the past being repeated in the present?

- What unmet needs in the past remain unmet in the present?

- What am I looking for from the Other in the here and now that I need to be giving to myself?

- What am I doing for the Other that I need to be doing for myself?

- How do I want the Other to be that I am afraid of being myself?

- To what degree have I remained enmeshed with one or both of my parents?

- What are the protective responses that I typically manifest in my relationship with the Other, particularly in times of conflict?

- To what degree do I own my own life and take conscious, loving responsibility for it in the here and now?

These are questions that are deep and challenging, and that need to be approached with compassion, sensitivity, empathy, kindness, care, patience and understanding. It is not easy to pursue such questions on your own, and it is wise to seek out somebody who is in a position to accompany you on the quest, and who can provide the safe emotional holding that will enable you to take the risk of embarking on that quest.

In What Ways Is The Past Being Repeated In The Present?

It is not an uncommon phenomenon that we become intimate with Another who relates in similar ways to those of a parent – ways that were threatening and that sent us creatively into hiding what was dangerous to show of our presence. It could be that you have married your mother or your father. It is also not uncommon to be attracted to someone whose behaviour is completely opposite to that of a parent whose unlived life made it dangerous for you to be present to your own precious life. The wisdom and hope in this attraction is that because the Other is so different in her or his behaviour, the likelihood is very low of the earlier abandonment being repeated. There is the added benefit that how the Other responds to you can seemingly mirror what you need to be doing for yourself.

However, the opposite behaviour is likely to be extreme and coming from a protective inner place in the Other who believes that he or she is meant to live life for you; what he or she is offering to you is absent in his or her own relationship with Self. For example, a woman whose father's relationship with her was fraught with aggression, impatience and narcissism may find herself attracted to Another who is over-pleasing, eternally patient and seemingly selfless. The woman, in her own relationship with herself, may unconsciously be repeating her father's behaviour and be aggressive, impatient and preoccupied with herself. She is likely also to be aggressive and over-demanding of her partner. This unhappy repetition within herself keeps alive what needs to come into consciousness. Her partner's protective behaviour colludes with her protective strategies and cleverly keeps at bay – until ready to face it – the pain of what happened in her relationship with her father, and with her mother who did not shield her from her father, and to find her own open care of herself in the here and now. Her Other equally needs to come into consciousness of the hurts experienced in his or her childhood which led to abandonment of Self in favour of others, and to find ways of being strongly there for Self now, rather than trying to live life for others.

Some examples are given below of what could be an endless list of behaviours from the Other in your current life which may echo those of a parent or other significant person in your early holding worlds:

▶ Suffocation of your individuality

▶ Helplessness

▶ Passivity

▶ Endless complaining

▶ Silent treatment

▶ Manipulation

▶ Comparison with others

▶ Lack of affection

▶ Dominance

▶ Controlling

▶ Narcissism

▶ Violence

▶ Addiction to work

▶ Addiction to substances

◗ Indecisiveness

◗ Irritability

◗ Impatience

◗ Chronic anxiety

◗ Chronic ill-health

◗ Depression

◗ Enmeshment with parents

When you feel sufficiently safe in yourself, it can be powerful for you to start taking note of the suffering, troubling behaviours and experiences from earlier life that are being repeated in the here and now, or those behaviours and responses from the Other that are exaggeratedly opposite to earlier experiences. The power lies in being able consciously to avail of the opportunities present in the here and now couple relationship to move towards being real and authentic, and so you may begin to see your partner as a separate Other (and, indeed, also the parent whose threatening behaviours are either being repeated or contradicted by your partner).

When consciousness arises, it does not judge the responses present – either of yourself, your partner or your parent – but it does seize the opportunities to gradually and solidly emerge in the face of those responses; liberation from a painful dependence now becomes possible for you. Such consciousness is also a wonderful gift to the Other, but will be received as such only when the Other is also on route to separateness.

Take the example of the man arriving at our practice in a highly anxious state arising (as he saw it) from the fact that his wife was planning to leave him and was no longer attracted to him. On the one hand, he idealised his wife in his life and, on the other hand, described how from the time they had first met she never stopped complaining, and that it was always 'her way or no way'. The seeming satisfaction with his wife was an unconscious rationalisation – an attempt to hold on to the relationship. The admission of her protective narcissism was a deflection from the deeper issue of poor intimacy with himself – an enmeshment with his mother and a terror of asserting his need to be true to himself. His protective goal was to find some way of holding on to his wife, and it was a painful realisation for him that it was his relationship with himself that urgently required attention and to which he needed to hold on.

What Unmet Needs From The Past Remain Unmet In The Present?

Unconditional love is the deepest need of each and every one of us; the essence of this love is a sense of awe in the face of the uniqueness and particularity of the presence of every person. In unconditional love, there is no confusion of the person with any of the expressions of the Self; there is no confusion with what you do, do not do, achieve or not achieve. There is nowhere else for such love to begin but within yourself; furthermore, the love you find in yourself is the source of your love for the Other. Yet, the human tragedy is that the majority of us find it very frightening to look to ourselves as the fountain of love, and we protectively attempt to draw it from Another by fair means or foul.

Unconditional love for your unique, sacred and precious presence in the world gets expressed in a myriad of everyday experiences, a few examples of which are listed below. Reflect for yourself to what extent these needs were unmet in the past and may be still unmet in the present:

- Experiencing belief in you, being trusted

- Being cherished

- Being supported

- Being encouraged

- Being 'got'/understood in your particularity

- Being listened to

- Being seen for yourself

- Experiencing kindness, patience

- Being encouraged to explore, to take risks, to be adventurous

- Being allowed to be different, to have one's own opinions and beliefs

- Being allowed to fail, and to succeed

- Being allowed to have one's own friends

- Being allowed to say no

- Being allowed the full range of feelings – both welfare and emergency

- Being allowed to make your own decisions and choices

- Being allowed to play

- Being allowed to be sick

- Being allowed to speak the truth

- Recognition that your felt experience is the most important information about yourself

It is not an easy process for any of us to travel the backroads of our childhoods, to bring into our conscious awareness what deep needs were unmet and how, incredibly, in the present we have unconsciously found a way to have that tragic past repeated in the here and now relationship. The Self does not let up in its quest for conscious wholeness, and the almost miraculous repetition of the dark past provides the path to reclaiming what were and are our just desserts – unconditional love and the safety to reside in the house of our own individuality – and give expression, physically, sexually, emotionally, socially, behaviourally, intellectually and creatively, to the unique and unrepeatable presence that is each one of us. The challenge of conscious wholeness is met primarily in the present in our relationship with ourselves, and in bringing our fullness to another, and in establishing definite and clear boundaries around our birthright to be true to ourselves, and, out of that ground, to also be true to the Other.

What Am I Seeking From The Other That I Need To Be Giving To Myself?

The answer to the question "what am I seeking from the Other that I need to be giving to myself?" will, almost certainly, unearth memories of what you were looking for from your parents and did not get, and what you are now hoping to receive from the Other. At an unconscious level, you are likely to be looking to the Other to do for you what your parents did not do – essentially to take responsibility for your wellbeing. In an adult-adult relationship, this is a recipe for interruption – interruption that is necessary – because the truth is you need no longer be dependent on having parents. You are now an adult who can, as consciousness arises, take charge of your own life – and you can become very skilful at doing so, much better than parents or any others, who do not have access to all the inside information that you possess.

The Other does you no favours if she or he takes on responsibility for your life, but it would certainly be loving of you if she or he were kindly and compassionately to challenge your dependence. But the reality is that you will attract a person who has as much emergence to do as yourself and, as a result, it can be a case of the blind leading the blind until conscious enlightenment begins to occur for either one of you.

As children, we are dependent on our parents, and other significant adults, to provide us with care. The most obvious need is our need for physical care, but we need care around all the expressions of Self: physical, sexual, emotional, social, behavioural, intellectual and creative. The most important issue is the emotional context in which any such care is given. For example, you may have received good physical care in the sense of diet, hygiene, clothing, health needs, but if that care was provided in a cold, dutiful, functional, abstracted manner, then you will not have experienced it as loving responsiveness to you. Essentially, we need from our parents both heart and head care, and we need that care consistently and persistently.

Heart care can be described as:

- Embracing
- Holding
- Tender
- Compassionate
- Warm
- Receptive
- Sensitive
- Heartfelt
- Gentle

Head care might be described as:

▶ Championing

▶ Supporting

▶ Encouraging

▶ Believing in

▶ Solving problems

▶ Making decisions

▶ Guiding

▶ Identifying need

One without the other is not real care: if there is heart for me in my need but no active responsiveness – no head care – then I am left with my need. If there is attempt at action without the crucial information on my actual care needs that comes from heart care, then the action is highly unlikely to be effective. As an adult, you need to find that heart and head care for yourself. There is wonderful security in the realisation that you can give yourself the loving responsiveness to need that you yearn for and deserve; you have all the resources to do so – you have the heart and you have the head! You can be the ideal, loving parent – mother and father – to yourself now that your actual parents were not able to be because of their interrupted relationships with themselves.

What is important here is finding the safety and support to notice for yourself what you may be expecting from your partner but need to be giving to yourself and, naturally, from that place of independence to receive graciously from your Other when she or he is in the open place to give unconditionally. All the time you need to be mindful that where you are is where you need to be; there is no wrong or bad place for you to be, but there are necessarily creative, protective places from which most of us regularly operate. Any criticism from yourself, or perceived criticism from the Other only reinforces the protective walls. Even to get as far as taking note of what is missing and what you need to find for yourself demonstrates that some level of holding is present.

With regard to the Other, you can only surmise what unsayables or undoables are being masked by his or her protective behaviours; only the Other can tell you the truth about what lies hidden. We use the phrase 'perceived criticism' to represent the internalisation of what Another says or does. The truth is you are not the target of the Other's criticism; everything the Other says is totally about that person, and is business for the Other to deal with, not your business.

When you are separate and independent, you are in that solid place to hear what the Other says or does as being completely about him or her. From a place of care, you might gently enquire: "How is it that you are saying what you are saying, or not doing what you really want to do?" If the Other's verbal or physical behaviour threatens your wellbeing, you need to safeguard your presence with a definite verbal or behavioural response without diminishing in any way the Other's presence. For example, if your partner is aggressively shouting at you, you could communicate in word and action: "Right now, I'm feeling unsafe, and I'm removing myself from the threat of your behaviour, for my sake and also for your sake."

What Am I Doing For The Other That I Need To Be Doing For Myself?

The question "what am I doing for the Other that I need to be doing for myself?" is the flip-side of the question discussed above. So, intelligently, we project what we need to be doing for ourselves by either doing it for others or by getting them to do it for us. There are many people who unconsciously dedicate their lives to the service of others, exhausting themselves in trying to identify and satisfy the multiple and varied needs of others – for example, parents, partners, children, friends. This is a powerful substitute means of gaining recognition, of having a sense of worth, of being of value and significance, but there is no rest from it because the terror is always there that any failure to meet the needs of the Other will result in rejection – a fate worse than death itself in the experience of the child, and a sense carried into adulthood. A phrase commonly heard is: "She/ he killed herself/himself for others" – an apt phrase because the hunger and thirst for love fears not death but rejection.

Each individual will have their own response, but it is likely you will see yourself in some of the examples below of the ways in which we can find ourselves compulsively putting our lives at the service of others' needs – needs that urgently require attention in our own lives. We stress here the word 'compulsively', this indicating that the supposed care we are offering to others is not coming from an unconditional, open, free place but from fear and conditionality. The hidden unconscious agenda is: "If I do all this for you, won't you see how good and lovable I am, and return the same unstinting care?"

- Consideration only of the Other, none for yourself
- Identifying the Other's needs with no thought for your own needs
- Satisfying the Other's needs at the sacrifice of self-care
- Nurturance of the Other at neglect of yourself

▶ Taking responsibility for the Other and
   abandoning yourself

▶ Attentiveness to the Other and deafness to yourself

▶ Rescuing the Other at risk to yourself

▶ Generosity towards the Other with meanness
   towards yourself

When expressions of care come from an unconditional place, they have a very different quality – both for the giver and for the receiver – than when they come from the driven place in us, and we feel that difference when we are safe enough to check in with the truth of our felt experience. It can be quite shocking and a very painful realisation for those of us who have been apparently selfless to discover that not only has all our endless doing for the Other never been good enough, but also that our blindness to care for ourselves maintained a starvation for love. Certainly, the over-attending to the Other has an important substitute purpose, but it can never meet our deepest longing – unconditional love for Self.

There is no doubt but that these are painful realisations, but without the pain you would never uncover what you truly deserve – consciousness of your innate lovability and worthiness of care. It is also a suffering when you become conscious that you cannot do for the Other what he or she needs to do for themselves; a suffering that can be alleviated by the realisation that when you take on that task, you are lost to yourself and not really present to the Other. When you take on conscious responsibility for your own life, which is your most sacred responsibility, you bring your full and real presence to the Other – an amazing gift. The shift here is from "I will mend your life" to "I will mend my own life, and thereby take that impossible responsibility off your shoulders and, in doing so, I am free to support you in your mending of your life." The emerging consciousness of the creativity, endless resourcefulness, understanding, compassion and self-support that belong to each of you accelerates the emergence of the Real Self both for you and your partner.

How Do I Want the Other to Be that I Am Afraid to Be Myself?

You have seen in Chapter Five how in the early stages of relationship we are often drawn to another who is very different from us in their characteristics and ways of being. The unconscious meaning and purpose to such attraction of opposites is that the Other mirrors for me what I most experienced in early interruptions, and my responses then are what protected me, and continue to protect me in the here and now adult intimate relationship. In the later stages of the relationship, another dynamic of opposites can begin to emerge whereby I try to get the Other to be in the world in ways that I myself need to be but am too afraid to be.

The deep desire to express the fullness of who you are in the intimate relationship can be assisted in coming into the open through the process of consciously noting the behaviours you dare not show but that the Other apparently has no problems in expressing. We use the word 'apparently' because it is usually the case that the Other's behavioural expression is also coming from a protective rather than from an open place and is exaggerated, and thereby threatening, in nature; both partners are operating at the extreme ends of the continuum. Some examples are given below of the kinds of pairing of opposites that can occur:

Partner A	**Partner B**
It Is 'Taboo' to	**'Dares' to**
Be different	*Be rebellious*
Express individuality	*Be oppositional*
Attend to self	*Be 'all about me'*
Have time for self	*Insist 'my time is mine'*
Express own values	*Impose own values*
Be decisive	*Be defiant*
Be independent	*Need nobody*
Express anger	*Be volatile*
Look for love	*Insist on 'love'*
Say 'no'	*Rigidly sticks to 'no'*
Have own opinions	*Be opinionated*
Pursue own chosen career	*Put career above all else*
Choose own interests	*Insist own interests come first*

Interruptions occur when both of you in the relationship are operating at protective extremes. What is being called for is to find the safety to make the shift from being walled off at the extremes to building bridges that connect you to one another, these bridges being built when you emerge from the hidden place into being fully yourself. It is of note that even though the two of you are expressing opposite protective behaviours, what lies hidden behind the protective walls of you both, and that is seeking to emerge into the light, are the same natural human qualities that belong to all of us.

What Lies Hidden For Both

- Our uniqueness
- Our individuality
- Our worthiness of being attentive to ourselves

- Our worthiness of having time for ourselves
- The rightness of having our own beliefs, opinions, interests, perspectives
- Our integrity
- Our worthiness of seeking love from others
- Our birthright to be authentic
- The rightness of being independent, of living one's own life
- The rightness of our emotions – welfare and emergency

It is important to distinguish between the unconscious projective dynamic at play when the two people are operating at opposite poles of behaviour, and that leads to interruptions, and the open relating that occurs when two individuals are very different from one another in their ways of being but are both operating from an inner place of security. Conscious differences reveal our individuality and can be a very creative force in an intimate relationship, emphasising the mystery of each person's uniqueness and thereby adding to the adventure of the relationship. There are, of course, also situations where difference in a couple can result in them consciously, and benignly, choosing to part but remain friends, if not intimates; for example, differences in preference of where to live, differences in regard to the desire for children, differences in the kind of lifestyles that are fitting for each one.

When the unconscious dynamic of projection is at play, interruptions inevitably occur – the attraction of opposites begins to show cracks. The question is often put to us as to whether it is better not to rock the boat if the power of opposites maintains a protective status quo. But while the interplay of opposites has a purpose, a protective stalemate means that neither partner is living their own precious life and continues to live fearfully, rather than joyfully and playfully. While there is a certain comfort in being hidden, it is a tragedy not to emerge into the light of consciousness of the wholeness and fullness of your wondrous nature. Furthermore, where there are children – as you have seen – the unlived lives of the parents will seriously interrupt the emergence of the children's wholeness and fullness.

To What Degree Have I Remained Enmeshed With My Parents?

Many an intimate relationship becomes interrupted, and sometimes broken, by one partner's enmeshment with his or her family of origin; this enmeshment on one partner's part often accompanied by estrangement from family of origin on the other partner's part. A not untypical example is where the woman in the relationship spends more time on the phone and in the home of her parents than she does with her male partner who, in turn, has no time for her family and no contact with his own family of origin. Typically, the man's reaction in this situation is to feel rejected by his partner and to be dismissive of her over-involvement with her family. He keeps his hurt hidden, and she reads his criticism as a rejection of her.

In this mutually protective situation, the relationship can quickly deteriorate. Even though the relationship may be deeply unhappy, neither of the partners possesses enough inner security to challenge the interruption, and so the years may roll on with no breakthrough occurring for either person.

Enmeshment means continuing co-dependence and restricted lives. When you find the safety to consciously investigate the nature of your present contact with members of your family of origin, and the degree of enmeshment or separateness that characterises that contact, then you are taking a powerful step towards strengthening the relationship with yourself and, by extension, with the Other with whom you are seeking intimacy. Enmeshment with family of origin can get expressed in many ways, such as those described below:

⚬ Still living with parents and dependent on their approval for how you live your life

⚬ Living apart from parents but making very frequent phone contact and visits to them, and needing their approval

⚬ No physical contact but blaming parents, or siblings, for your past and present suffering

⚬ Living apart but making obligatory, hostile visits, also feeling very let down by parents

⚬ Living apart from parents and wanting no contact whatsoever with them

Enmeshment means lack of presence to the Other; you are still turned towards a parent rather than cleaving to your Other. Presence is the essence of intimacy – that is how we get to know one another in a relationship. Boundaries are very important for the safe holding of the intimate two-person relationship. Boundaries ensure that it is a couple relationship where the two partners can be present to one another, and to their children if they start a family of their own, without the distraction of a third party, parent or sibling, also active in their emotional space. When you are needing to make choices and decisions, to take action for your everyday wellbeing, your primary consideration – after your own inner considerations – needs to be the person with whom you are sharing your life.

When a third adult is intruded into the considerations of the intimate couple relationship, then interruption inevitably occurs; communication gets muddied, the intimate partners are not present to one another in the way that is needed for intimacy, there is the experience of being overlooked, the experience of one's needs and desires and viewpoint being overridden by the needs, desires and viewpoint of the intruding parent or sibling. If you find yourself in the situation where the Other is looking away from you, you are likely to adopt the protective strategy of either absenting yourself from the couple, fighting your partner on his or her involvement with family of origin, fighting his or her family of origin, or turning yourself inside out to seduce the Other away from those people who seem be grabbing all his or her attention.

The hidden truth seeking to emerge into the open for the enmeshed partner is: "I am my own person, I deserve and am able to stand on my own two feet, living life from my centre". For the Other caught up in the interrupted relationship the truth needing to emerge is: "I deserve and desire the wholehearted presence and attention of the person with whom I'm sharing my life; I deserve to be known". Ultimately, we each need to be married to ourselves for our marriage with another to thrive. You can really see the Other only when you are standing separate in your own space.

When you come into consciousness that you are here to live your own marvellous life, and not there to live the lives of others – parents, siblings or partner – you will find that you care about them, that you have understanding and compassion when they remain stuck behind their protective walls, but you realise that you need to stay separate, and not in any way compromise your hard-earned separateness, and the freedom that comes from that separateness. If they remain hostile and threatening, you need to establish very definite boundaries to safeguard your wellbeing and integrity, and you need to be firm that you remain open, but only to safe contact with them.

The goal of adulthood is freedom from painful enmeshment with parents, siblings and others, not reconciliation! There is no doubt that, for each one of us, establishing our separateness – particularly from parents – is one of our greatest challenges, and one for which we need all the support we can get. We believe that the intimate couple relationship can evolve to be the most powerful ground on which to establish that necessary separateness. Certainly, when a couple truly realise that all-one-ness is fundamental to our wellbeing, they are ready to support each other in the quest of finally flying the family nest. But when that support is not present within the couple, then it is important that it is found elsewhere.

What Particular Protective Responses Are Manifesting In The Relationship?

The history of internal interruptions that we bring to our relationship with the Other gets manifested in the protective strategies that we each employ in our interactions with one another; the protectors of each of us tending to be at opposite ends of a continuum. The wisdom in being with someone whose survival strategies are different from yours is that similarity of protectors would be highly threatening: the resultant clash and competition for survival would be too hard to sustain. Some examples of how couples employ protective strategies that click together to create a protective dance that works – at least to the extent of keeping us safe until the time comes when we have sufficient safety to shift from protectiveness to openness and realness – are given over.

Partner A	Partner B
Passivity	Desire to be needed
Guilt	Avoidance of complaint
Sense of responsibility for the Other	Tendency to yield
Abandonment of Self	Tendency to be elusive
Compulsion to live life for the Other	Aggression
Perfectionism	Sense of entitlement
Failure to ask anything for Self	Abrogation of responsibility for Self
Narcissism	Desire to be cared for
Push for the Other to live life for him or her	Tendency to complain
Carelessness	Stubbornness
Tendency to be demanding	Possessiveness

Whatever end of the continuum you may find yourself coming from, what is being revealed is your fear of taking conscious responsibility for your own life. The depth of the protective reactions reveals the depth of the interruptions each of you has experienced in your first relationships, and internalised in your relationships with yourselves. When opposite protectors are present, both fearful partners have a chance of getting some comfort from their different strategies. Of course, the ultimate purpose of the relationship is to move from the unconscious world of illusion to realisation, from surviving to thriving, from dependence to independence, from fearfulness to security, and from conditional relating to unconditional love.

Protective strategies provide only some relief from the pain, this being a wise and loving way of keeping the issue alive because interruption will eventually occur and thereby provide the opportunity for consciousness to become present. The power of the presently occurring interruption is that it provides the opportunity for each partner to come in touch with their suffering and to get beneath to the real source of the suffering – which is not the other person – so that real responsiveness may take place. Making connection with present suffering leads the way to making a connection with deeper, older suffering that had to be hidden because it was too unbearable to face into; finding responsiveness to current suffering opens the way to responsiveness to historical suffering. If you can discover ways of responding to yourself in the current interruption, then that creates a sense of security, a sense of possibility that you may even be able to hold and respond to what hitherto had appeared unbearable.

Suppose you find yourself in a relationship interrupted by the Other's protector of excessive attention to other women or men, and your protective response is to withdraw into silence and be distant. It reduces suffering if you can find the safety to open up to and hold your felt experience in this situation – possibly an experience of hurt, loss, sadness, confusion, outrage – and find responsiveness to that felt experience. For example, noticing how important it is that you hold on to the truth of your power to attract, that you find appreciation of yourself, that you find interest in yourself, that you let the Other know what it feels like love to you, that you can declare your worthiness of having him or her present to you. It is important that you understand for yourself that his or her distraction on to others is business for the Other to deal with and not for you to change, or coax him or her out of, or control. You know the Other's reaction is no reflection on you. Your business is to shift from withdrawal to coming into the light of visibility and making yourself known – doing now what you understand for yourself to have been too threatening to do in early interrupted relationships.

When conflict does raise its head, there is likely to be an intensification of the protective reactions on both sides, as in the examples below.

Partner A	*Partner B*
Dissolving into tears	Verbal threats
Complete apathy	Violence
Retreat into helplessness	Staying with blame
Emotional withdrawal	Escalation of intrusiveness

These heightened reactions represent a last-ditch attempt to return the relationship to a protective even keel – what with consciousness would be more accurately seen as an 'evil kneel'. At this time, neither partner has yet found the solid ground to appreciate that it is in being separate that togetherness will be found. The safety needed for this emergence into conscious separateness is most likely to be found initially outside the relationship, but the hope is that eventually it will be found within each of them and, as a result, between them.

The power of the breakdown of the protective dance is that it opens up the space for something different to happen; if the dance is no longer happening, then both partners are thrown back on themselves and pushed to ask "what am I going to do now?" If safe holding comes from someplace – for example, a family member, friend, counsellor, through a book, a workshop, a lecture that resonates with you – then that question may be answered in a more open, loving manner than the protective dance could ever do. If there is no safety, then the likely answer will be to find another 'dance partner' as quickly as possible, as standing alone on the 'dance floor' feels too exposing, too vulnerable, too frightening.

If the dance is, for example, one of pushy blame and helpless retreat, in its breakdown there is an opportunity for the blaming partner to come back to Self and find the strong self-care that comes with taking responsibility for yourself. And there is an opportunity for the withdrawing partner to hold his or her own ground, strong in the knowledge that the Other's blaming protector belongs with the Other and is best sent back to him or her, strong in the truth that you are not responsible for the Other's reactions.

To What Degree Am I Taking Conscious Responsibility For My Own Life?

It is important to remember that when you operate from a protective place, you are still taking responsibility, but at an unconscious level, for your sacred life. You are reducing the threats to your presence in the best way you can, given the level of safety you feel. Conscious responsibility is the realisation that you need no longer be dependent on others; you can depend on yourself now and begin the exciting prospect of living your own life, from the inside out, from a soul place. This is a long road but in our core, in our soul or spirit, it is the road that we all want to travel. When two people in intimate relationship are on this road of ownership of their individual lives and have become the champions of each other's all-one-ness, then their couple relationship will blossom.

When you find the safety to take conscious responsibility for your own life, this is when your wellbeing is best safeguarded. Even with the best will in the world, the Other can never take care of your wellbeing in the way you can. You are the one with the access to all the relevant information, and you are the *only one* with this information because you are the only one who has lived through what your particular life-story has thrown up for you. You are the only one who knows all the sensitivities, all the nuances, all the detail of that story, and the felt experience of that story. Nobody but you can know, for example, what it was like to grow up with a father who constantly found you to be in the wrong, constantly found you to be 'an idiot' in the way you behaved. Nobody but you knows what that felt like for you and what you figured you had to do to survive such threats.

Nobody knows what particular interruptions ensued in your relationship with yourself, what aspects of yourself you kept hidden, and what responsiveness is needed now in order for you to find the safety to dare again to give full expression to your individuality, to your intelligence, to your capability.

Chapter Seven

Breakthrough To Being Me

Safe Holding Is Crucial To Breakthrough From Interruptions

Whether or not you can use the power of any interruption that may turn up in your intimate couple relationship depends on the level of safe holding that exists within each of you and between you. Safe holding refers to the kind of atmosphere that surrounds you whereby it is safe to be yourself and to give full expression to all the dimensions of your unique presence.

Some individuals who have suffered severe interruptions in their earlier lives have had to bury their sense of uniqueness and sacredness and will describe themselves as "a nothing", or will say "I hate myself", or "nobody would want me", or "I'm despicable." Such individuals have had to extinguish their light in the face of annihilating interruptions, where their very presence was rubbished or enslaved or constantly violated or ignored, or never held or nurtured. It is a monumental challenge for such a person ever again to trust another, and he or she necessarily will keep repressed and buried his or her real Self.

Long-term therapeutic safe holding, by a highly conscious practitioner, is needed for this person to slowly but surely emerge from hiding. There is nothing more terrifying – and the terror is wise – than having to maintain little or no sense of one's Self. Those individuals for whom the experience of early interruptions was less severe will have some sense of substance, some sense of their unique presence in the world, but will suffer around particular expressions of the Self.

Take, for example, the woman who in her early life was compared unfavourably with a mother considered to be 'a beauty' and who, as a result, has doubts about her physical attractiveness and goes to great lengths to create the 'body beautiful'. Her protection is 'I am my body' and the underlying hope is 'if you find my body attractive, you'll be attracted to me'. The confusion of Self with physical appearance puts huge pressure on physical presence and weighs it down with the protective agenda of proving one's attractability and lovability, these being unassailable truths that do not need to be proved. The safety to be spontaneously physically expressive is now absent, and physical self-consciousness replaces open, free, joyous expression.

Clearly, when a relationship interruption is provoked by the Other, unless you are in a secure place in yourself, you will not be able to maintain expression of what has come under threat from the Other – your whole person or some particular expression of your Self. When you are not in a safe place in yourself – when you do not have that inner stronghold – one protective response to the interruption is introjection whereby you internalise the reactions of the Other that have led to the interruption as being about you.

Introjection is a frequent protector on the part of children who, of necessity, are dependent on parents and other significant adults in their holding worlds. For example, the child who is told aggressively "you're so stupid" will introject that message and, subsequently, find ways to reduce the threat to intellectual expression by, for example, perfectionism, or acting 'stupid', or by giving up all effort, or by becoming aggressive, so no one will dare to taunt him or her ever again. Unless the child begins to find the safe holding he or she deserves – love, encouragement, support, recognition of effort, emphasis on attainment, belief in his or her capability, making learning fun and an adventure – that child will continue to repress his or her natural curiosity, love and eagerness to learn. Without such safe holding, it would be dangerous for the child to contradict openly the message coming from the parent who is at the centre of the child's universe.

Safe Holding for the Different Expressions of Self

Your Self gets expressed in this world in a number of wonderful ways: physically, sexually, emotionally, behaviourally, intellectually, socially and creatively. You have seen in Chapter Four how interruptions can occur to those different expressions. Interruptions happen when your Self is confused, identified with any of these expressions. Conditionality enters in when you are loved not for your presence but for one of your expressions; for example, "I love you because you're so good to me"; "I love you because you make me proud"; or "I love you because you're beautiful" or "clever" or "popular" or "pleasing". It is crucial that each of your expressions of Self is met with safe holding so you can hold on to what is true for every one of us. Safe holding means recognition that these expressions are wonderful channels for us to experience human life, but they are not the measure of us:

- ◗ "I have a body but I'm not my body"
- ◗ "I have feelings but I'm not my feelings"

❱ "I have sexual energy but I'm not my sexuality"

❱ "I have intelligence but I'm not my intelligence"

❱ "I engage in behaviours but I'm not my behaviours"

❱ "I have the power to connect with others but I'm not my sociability"

❱ "I have creative powers but I'm not my creativity"

You take an important step towards that necessary inner stronghold when you come into consciousness of the extent to which you currently feel safe to be spontaneous in these different means of expression of your Self. For example:

❱ Do you feel physically confident?

❱ Do you feel free to own and express all feelings both welfare and emergency?

❱ Do you perceive your sexuality, your passion for life, as belonging to you and for your joy in life?

❱ Do you realise your genius?

❱ Do you know that all your behaviour makes sense?

❱ Do you cherish the unique presence you bring to others?

❱ Do you appreciate your boundless creativity?

Or is there threat present for you so that you find yourself disliking your body, repressing your feelings, feeling apathetic in your attitude to life, believing you are slow or 'just average', seeing yourself as a 'failure', as awkward socially, or as lacking creativity?

Safe Holding: Releasing The Power Of The Interruption

In order to release the power of whatever particular interruption arises in your present couple relationship, you need to have some sense that your felt experience in the situation will be safely held, and will be taken into account, and responded to with love. You are the only one who knows all that is arising in you in the interruption: what old threats are being triggered, what sensitivities are being touched, what fears, what anxieties, what confusions are there for you. In responding to the interruption in an open way, it is important to remind yourself that nobody else has a finger on the truth of you – no matter how much they might protectively proclaim that they have: "The trouble with you is..."; "you said that deliberately to hurt me"; "your problem is you're all me, me, me"; "you obviously still have unfinished business with your mother."

You are the only expert on you; you are the only one with all the relevant, correct, precise information on what is happening in your interior world. If you can connect with that information, stay with it, entertain it, take it on board, then you have the solid base for letting whatever may have been hidden to come to the surface. There is now safe holding for you; this is your security that there will be real care of you.

Making this breakthrough from protective care to real care when an interruption occurs is a major challenge and calls for much patience, compassion, kindness, deep reflection, querying, figuring things out, checking the evidence for what sits well and what does not fit for you. When we become familiar with this process of figuring out what real care feels and looks like, it no longer seems so daunting. The tragedy is that we are not given opportunities to practise this kind of care in our earlier lives and into our adulthood relationships; we do not have the chance to familiarise ourselves with it in the way that would make it straightforward and not fraught with fear. In adulthood, it is crucial that we pursue safe holding of ourselves – we need to start taking the risk of doing it. When we find some of that safe holding, interruptions are less terrifying.

Suppose, for example, you find yourself at the receiving end from the Other of harsh criticism that is conveyed in very definite, seemingly authoritative terms: "You knew that is a sensitive issue for me and yet you deliberately provoked me out of some twisted place that comes from your dysfunctional family background."

The felt experience in the face of such severe protective reactions from the Other can be deeply distressing and frightening. But if you can hold with yourself and not lose yourself to trying to manage the Other – to placate, appease, persuade, teach – then you have the possibility of discovering what is being called for in guarding your wellbeing. You will come in touch with the critical issues at stake – for example, the need for belief in you, the need for fairness, the need to be respected, the need to be understood as a good-hearted person, the need for a boundary around the sacredness of your own individual presence. These are important needs, and it is crucial that they do not get left in the hands of the Other, who is patently not in a position to respond.

These needs are best kept in your own hands, and if you find responsiveness to yourself, you have the safety – when things have calmed down – to let the Other know what it is you look for, and deserve, what is right for you, in the couple relationship. The interruption now has worked to bring you into closer connection with yourself, and stronger, more open care of you, and this, clearly, will have positive impact on what takes place between you and the Other. Because some of the protective reactions have been taken out of the space between you, there is more scope now for a bridge to be created, for openness and authenticity to emerge. Of course, there is no guarantee of this happening because it takes two to make an interlocking bridge, and the Other also has to find that inner safe holding for breakthrough.

The Ultimate Safe Holding Is Within Yourself

The degree to which there has been safe holding of us in childhood determines the extent of the challenge of finding, in adulthood, safe holding within ourselves. The ultimate safe holding *is* within ourselves; that is the only holding that we can actually count on to be always there, that can be persistent, consistent and continuous. No other being can do this for you, and it is not love to even try because it means the Other abandoning Self and her or his precious and sacred life. Relief, freedom, lightness and security come with the realisation that you are capable of creating that abiding stronghold – no longer any need to be dependent on others who, because of their own suffering and their own need for safeguarding, cannot provide it for you.

Separateness is a Crucial Dimension of Safe Holding

When we meet with protective behaviour in the Other – when we are faced with an interruption in the relationship – a typical response is to go into protective mode ourselves. The tendency is to leave ourselves and to focus on the Other and how she or he is behaving; we find ourselves fearfully trying to figure out how to manage the Other. We make their business our business, and we use their reactions as the criterion of whether we are doing right or not in the situation. For example, you meet with the unconscious protector from the Other of 'your job is to make me happy, and you're not doing a very good job of it, and that's why I'm distant from you'. The fear of such withdrawal can be profound when it carries reminders of early experiences of the withdrawal of love. You may find yourself turning yourself inside out to do the business of making the Other happy, at whatever cost to yourself.

The felt experience of this is one of invisibility, of being insubstantial, of the Other taking over all the space, of an inner void. You are lost to yourself and adrift in the Other's world where there is no space for you; it is not your world and it is not good for you to persist with attempts to act there. The very unhappy felt experience is your wisdom alerting you to the need to bring to the surface the truth that you have had to bury; this truth being that you are unreservedly deserving at all times of loving responsiveness to how life is for you.

The query for you in this example is how life is for you in the face of this protective push from the Other to live life for him or her. When there is some safety, if you can begin to take your eye off the Other and look to what is happening in your inner world – make the connection with all the feelings, needs, considerations arising for you – then you are dealing with what is properly your business, with the business that is worthy of you, the business for which you have all the information you need. When you make connection with all that is arising within you, then you can see clearly what needs to happen for the safeguarding of your unique and precious presence.

In the example above, you can see about making yourself visible, finding your sense of substance as a separate person in your own right, taking your rightful place in the world. When you engage with your proper business, then the experience shifts from a sense of void, blankness and darkness to fullness, aliveness and light. Clearly, when you are operating from a place of fullness, aliveness and light, you are in a position both to maintain your own 'I-land' and reach out to the Other – create your span of the bridge of connection – reach out to another 'I-land'.

The enormity of the shift from 'no-land' to an 'I-land' needs to be acknowledged and understood; the 'no-land' being what was offered to us as the price of conditional love, and living life for oneself having been simply out of the question. The tragedy is that when you are not allowed be your own 'I-land', in order to survive you try to colonise the Other's 'I-land', either through trying to live life for and through them, or through trying to get the Other to live life for and through you. The enormity of the quest involved calls for great compassion, patience, kindness and encouragement of ourselves – it truly is an heroic journey.

Daring To Say The Unsayable

Over many decades of practice, we have heard so many individuals, at the early stage of therapy, speak about what they dare not say or do about the very threatening behaviours they encounter daily in their intimate couple relationships.

A not uncommon revelation is: "I've been living in hell for many years in my marriage." Most frequently, hell is described as the Other's constant blaming, demanding, criticising, shouting, controlling, aggression and, sometimes, violence. These individuals have no consciousness at this early stage that the hell they have endured, and continue to endure, is not about the Other's threatening behaviour but about the painful disconnection from themselves that they made – out of necessity – many years before they met the Other. The unsayable that needs to be spoken certainly involves the Other's protective responses and, even more so, the projections and introjections of the significant adults in their childhood years. But the far more important unsayable is the truth of one's worthiness of unconditional love, at all times.

You can be sure that if, as an adult, you inhabit your own individuality, if you are independent and conscious that you have everything you need to safeguard yourself in the face of the threatening reactions of others, then you will not stay in hell for even five minutes. Your boundaries around care and nurturance of yourself will be firm and definite and, in very certain terms, you will communicate to the Other that you do not allow anybody to intimidate you into submissiveness. You will do this with conscious words and actions, where you speak from the separate place of 'I', and the safeguarding actions you take will be about you and for you, and not against the Other or his or her unconscious interruptions of the relationship. Easier written than done! But make no mistake about it, you have managed to survive the slings and arrows of outrageous misfortune to date, and the same intelligence and creativity that went into developing your protective walls are available for your emergence into fullness, and for you to begin to build bridges rather than walls with others who are in a position to reciprocate.

When one partner unconsciously believes that the Other is responsible for his or her misery, the projection of blame is as much an interruption to the relationship as are the Other's protective reactions. As long as each of them continues to try to make the other responsible for their mutual unhappiness, the relationship will spiral into more and more interruptions. The escalation of interruption that happens when each is stuck in blame mirrors the depth and breadth of the disconnection from Self within each, and is crying out to be seen and understood for what it is so that it may be resolved.

Saying the Unsayable: the Interruption of the Affair

A particular interruption that is often greatly feared, and seen as something from which there can be no return, is where one of the partners starts to have an affair. There is no doubt that the level of protectiveness underlying the affair is severe, but it has the same meaning and potential power as any other interruption. Because an affair, by its very nature, is secretive, hidden, duplicitous, it indicates that the individuals involved are acting from a Screen Self. When any one of us is operating from the fear-laden Screen Self, our protective reactions inevitably cause distress and unhappiness for others in a relationship with us. So, if you find yourself in relationship with Another who is having an affair, there is no doubt that you will need to find strong holding of yourself to manage the pain, and find the power of the interruption. The Other will also need to find this safe holding if she or he is to find the deeper understanding of themselves that is being called for through the protective behaviour of the affair.

You are likely to find that your initial reaction is to disconnect from yourself, and go right over into the Other's space – blaming, judging, rejecting, castigating, accusing. Even if there is an attempt on the Other's part to end the affair, to 'mend' the situation, you may find yourself questioning: "How can I ever trust you again?" You may find yourself checking the Other's every movement and whereabouts. You may find yourself obsessing about the third person involved – what that person might have that you haven't got, what is their attraction? You may find yourself wanting to hurt, destroy, kill one or other or both of them. You may find yourself apparently wanting to have nothing more to do with the Other but yet you cannot let go and are still embroiled in what can feel like a duel.

It is a huge challenge to find your way back home to yourself, to find a way of taking your sights off the Other and back on to yourself, but it is crucial that you do so. It is crucial to come into touch with your lived experience – hurt, loss, confusion, fear of abandonment, sense of betrayal, outrage, grief, bewilderment, shock. When you come in touch with, and hold, your lived experience, you can open up the possibility of finding real care and responsiveness for you (and you also give the Other the best chance she or he is going to have of going inwards and reflecting on what lies hidden under the protective behaviour of the affair).

The issue is no longer about trusting the Other but about trusting yourself; trusting yourself to see whatever comfort, solace, kindness you can find for yourself, trusting yourself to identify the important needs at stake for you. For example, to feel cherished, to be enjoyed for your unique presence, to be valued, to be visible – trusting yourself to let yourself be known in what works for you in the relationship and what is worthy of you; trusting yourself to make whatever requests you need to make; trusting yourself to establish boundaries that safeguard your separate presence. In other words, you are relating to yourself in the way you would like your partner to relate to you: with respect, care, responsiveness and understanding.

In particular, you need to trust yourself that you will keep checking in with yourself as to how you are experiencing the relationship with the Other. Checking to see if there is sufficient safety, sufficient sense that the Other too is reflecting and using the power of the interruption to emerge more into the open, sufficient sense of being on a shared journey, sufficient sense of shared compassion, understanding and kindness to continue journeying together. If the felt experience is of too much unsafety, then you trust yourself too to make the necessary decision to part ways.

Saying the Unsayable: the Interruption of Violence

Some interruptions occur at a more covert level – for example, the interruption caused by passivity – while others, such as that caused by physical, verbal or sexual violence, are more outwardly obvious and, as a result, attract more notice, and also more castigation.

When someone behaves in a violent fashion – physical, verbal, emotional or sexual – towards another, clearly that person's inner world is deeply dark, reflecting earlier interruptions of a severe nature. There are huge challenges involved for the person exhibiting violent behaviour to uncover what aspect of his or her true nature has had to be so deeply buried. Such an undertaking calls for very strong holding from someone outside the couple relationship, someone who is sufficiently seated in his or her own inner stronghold to be able to hold up a very firm boundary whereby violent reactions from the other are simply not an option.

The double tragedy in a relationship characterised by violence is that the other partner is operating from an equally dark inner world where having a strong sense of the sacredness of one's separate presence has been deeply buried, and where the setting of strong boundaries is simply undoable. This too reflects serious interruptions in earlier life, and this partner would also need very strong outside holding in order to begin to reclaim the truth of the integrity of her or his individual presence in the world, worthy at all times of persistent, consistent safeguarding action. It may be too unsafe for the partner subjected to violent behaviour to give the Other a chance to work out what the power of the violent protective reactions might be, and the power of the interruption for him or her might be to make a firm decision to no longer expose himself or herself to such threat and danger. Even with an ending of the intimate couple relationship, the crucial issues for each partner continue to be about finding their own respectful, caring, responsive relationship with Self.

Seeking Outside Safe Holding

In the situation where one or both partners have little sense of safe holding within themselves, it becomes necessary to find safe holding outside the intimate couple relationship if they are to be able to realise the power of whatever interruptions are arising in the here and now. It is usually the case that when one of an unhappy pair seeks therapy, that partner – most frequently the woman in an opposite gender relationship – will truly believe that it is the Other's behaviours that are interrupting the relationship. At this initial stage, this is her best option because the realisation that she has as deep inner work to do for herself as does the Other would be too scary to face. She will begin to face the reality only when she finds the safe holding of unconditional love, non-judgment, compassion and understanding – not just for herself but also for the Other, who undoubtedly is also in considerable turmoil.

We are sometimes asked if there is any point in just one of the partners seeking the safety needed to begin to emerge.

There can be a concern that taking a unilateral decision to seek outside professional help would be threatening for the Other, and only lead to an intensification of whatever conflict is present. Certainly, in our experience, the partner who is reluctant to come for help can express strong hostility towards the psychotherapist, and can be dismissive, sarcastic, or aggressively sceptical of the therapeutic process. We understand these responses to be further evidence of this partner's unhappy disconnection from Self. If he or she were in a more secure place, they would show interest in the Other's search; they would be open to listening to the Other's experience of personal therapy; they would be open to exploring any differences in beliefs that are present. Of course, if the person seeking help had a partner who was in such an open place, it is unlikely she would feel the need for professional holding because there would be sufficient safety in the intimate couple relationship for her to explore her inner turmoil.

If you find yourself in the situation where the Other attempts to disrupt your efforts to seek safe holding outside the couple relationship, it is important that you persist in your endeavour; remember it is not the relationship with the Other that primarily needs attention but your relationship with yourself. The crucial question is not, as you might initially believe, "how can I live with my partner?" but "how can I live with myself?" It is the marriage with yourself and your own commitment to your wellbeing that is crying out for attention. When this inner relationship begins to deepen, it is more likely that the space between the two of you will open up, allowing a move from dependence to independence.

Whether or not this opening up occurs, you need to persist with the deepening of the relationship with yourself. Nobody – least of all you – will gain with a return to the status quo in the couple relationship, and that includes any children who may be involved. The notion that a couple stays together, and should stay together, for the sake of children is an unconscious ploy that effectively interrupts the examination by each partner of their unlived lives. Children know when their parents are truly together and when they are play-acting at being together. Furthermore, the evidence suggests that children benefit more from living with one conscious parent rather than two unconscious parents. When one or both parents begin to live their unique lives, then the children have the safety to do likewise.

If you decide to seek holding outside your intimate relationship, remember that there are no prescriptions for finding the safety to be authentically yourself. In the prescription of techniques and advice giving, there is an implicit criticism which is an interruption in itself, and so does you no service in your attempts to respond to the couple interruption that is present. Prescriptions – which almost always have 'side-effects' – and advice, which adds 'vice' to an already difficult situation, fail to accept you where you are and the magic wisdom of that place. The very acknowledgement and exploration of the creativity of your protective walls provide a safe holding that you may never previously have experienced. Uninterrupted listening to your story, an awe response to how you have survived, and the wonder of how you found the 'perfect partner' for consciousness of all that has been, and needed to be, hidden to come into the light, these are the responses that provide the safe holding that can be life-changing.

The Chinese word for 'crisis' has a two-fold meaning – problem and opportunity – and so it is with a relationship interruption which can be described as an emergency, signalling alarm and also acting as the impetus for something that has been hidden to emerge. Emergence occurs spontaneously as safe holding deepens, just in the same way that being hidden happened spontaneously when, under threat, you created your protective walls and consequent relationship interruptions.

Such safe holding is not always easy to find. Furthermore, you may experience fear at the prospect of reaching out authentically to another, such fear ranging from minor to terror depending on the nature, frequency, intensity and endurance of the threats experienced over the course of your life. As adults, whom can we trust to speak openly about our suffering, and what it masks, when the most important people in our early lives were not in a conscious place to hold us? Nonetheless, at a covert level, we ceaselessly seek safety. The challenge is two-fold: firstly, everybody else is also seeking safety and, secondly, another – friend, colleague, medical doctor, manager, lover, psychotherapist – can provide only the level of safety that they have in their own interior world.

Unless matters have transformed in your family of origin, it is unlikely that you will find the safety there that supports you in speaking the truth of your experience and in taking conscious responsibility now for your sacred and precious life. It has been said that 'friendship is God's apology for family', and it is, indeed, in friendship that we can sometimes find solace, comfort and inspiration. If you choose to attend a psychotherapist or relationship counsellor, it is the depth of the relationship between you and the therapist or counsellor that will determine the extent of the safety you experience. Psycho-social helpers are human too and have had, and still have, their own suffering, and they can offer holding only to the extent of the level of consciousness they have achieved and the depth of their own relationship with Self. The crucial factor is the depth of the therapeutic relationship, since it is relationship interruptions in the first place that make for a perilous world for you to be yourself, so it is a relationship characterised by unconditional love, non-judgment, compassion, understanding and belief which makes an exciting, sacred and safe world for you to break through into fullness.

Whoever it is you choose to accompany you on your quest for emergence into wholeness, the Other can never promise you that their own fears and protectors will not arise in the therapeutic relationship. Nobody can promise to never feel impatient, to never want you to get to a particular place, to never wish that you would finally come to a 'resolution'. But what can be promised – and it is essential that it be promised to you – is that as a therapist I will continuously reflect on what is arising in me, and take ownership and responsibility for whatever is arising, so that I will not bring to you what does not belong to you, and so will not cause interruption in the relationship with you.

Wisely, you may start your search for safe holding where the threat seems low – for example, reading books on relationship, joining a course on self-development, talking with your family doctor, friends or others who are also experiencing challenges in their intimate relationships. Your first step may be tentative whereby with any hint of judgment, advice or irritability, you retreat speedily behind your protective walls. The hope is that you will find sufficient safety to try again or perhaps some other person will notice your retreat and accompany you with patient kindness.

Chapter Eight

How Do We Get It Together Now?

Getting It Together Now

The foundation for getting it together now with the Other is recognition and acknowledgement of the fact that you both are going through the same fundamental processes. You both have stories in which you experienced threat to the open, full expression of your individual presence in the world; you both wisely, and of necessity, created your protective strategies in the face of such threat. You both learned to hide aspects of yourself, and you both need safe holding in order to let your Real Self emerge, and find the conscious self-reliance and self-responsibility that enable you to take the risk of opening up to intimacy with Another. You both are deserving of compassion for what life has thrown up for you, and what you have had to do to survive the threats and dangers you have experienced.

In relationship with Another, there occurs an interplay of each of your repertoires of protective reactions; there occurs a defensive dance until safety starts to grow whereby there is conscious awareness of your protective behaviours, and understanding of their underlying source and meaning. Conscious awareness and conscious responsiveness enable you to shift from being locked together in a protective dance to accompanying one another as each of you dances to your own authentic tune – a shift to real intimacy.

Finding the safety to use the power of the present interruption is not easy, and you may need outside holding in order to disentangle from one another and come back into your own separate space. You may need an outside therapeutic relationship that provides the safe holding that enables you to reflect on your story, where you feel you can be heard in the reality of your felt experience without judgment, where you will find encouragement and support in taking the risk of emerging more from the hidden place into the light.

There are no prescriptions or proscriptions for how a couple who have become protectively alienated should get it together now. The real response is the uncovering of the creative inscriptions – the internalisation of the interruptions experienced in childhood – that will keep attempting to come to the surface and into the light.

When an intimate relationship has experienced intense and frequent interruptions that have endured over many years, it is often the case that too much hurtful water has gone under the bridge of the relationship and eroded any feelings the two people may have had for each other. Sometimes, leaving such a relationship – consciously making a decision to leave – may be the breakthrough opportunity presented by the relationship

The child cannot ever divorce the parents who, unwittingly, have made his or her life a hell, but the person in adult years does not have to be in such an enmeshed and dependent place, and can come to assert and take action on the truth that 'I deserve better'. The adult too can consciously realise that the partner who stands by me at all times is my Self, and that I can give to myself all that love and care that those others –

parents, teachers, peers, present partner – were not, and now are not, in the consciously secure place to provide for me.

This is consciousness at its most powerful – where you become the guardian of your own wellbeing, and a relationship with Another is a wonderful bonus but not a must in life. This is the meaning of aloneness; aloneness is not to be confused with isolation. Being all-one with myself does not mean that I will not experience the need for company, the need to sit with, experience and be close to Another. Being at one with myself means that when loneliness arises and prompts the need to be with Another, my response to that need comes from an inner stronghold and is not driven by the unconscious urge to own, control, be dependent on, or possess the Other.

Couples often believe that once interruptions start to occur, that is the end of the relationship. But many troubled relationships are redeemable; ways can be found of responding to interruptions that enable the free-flow again of love and the continuing emergence of individuality. Frequently used protective responses are: "we've fallen out of love", "he is not the person I married", "we're not compatible", "that's the way I am; don't ask me to change", "you've changed." These responses block any possibility of investigating the potential of the relationship, and come from the fear of facing the challenges involved in any such real investigation – essentially the challenge of looking at oneself and one's own relationship with Self.

You Always Are Where You Need To Be

In our practice, we hold strongly with the view that you always are where you need to be; you are always doing the best you can, given the level of safety, to take care of yourself. If you find yourself acting from within the unconscious world of protectors, remember that this is you taking care of yourself, trying to navigate the ocean of threats – the protectors of others – you may be encountering daily. The threats do not decrease as we move out from early childhood worlds; on the contrary, the threats increase the more we move out from the holding world of family to the wider holding worlds of peers, community, school, education and training settings, workplace and religion settings.

We believe – and we experience this in ourselves and in others – that nobody wants to stay hidden behind the walls of their protectors, but finding the safety to emerge from behind these walls is a difficult quest. In any intimate relationship, both partners are going to have their Shadow Selves so that the 'I' and the 'Thou' are forever encountering each other's protective worlds. Dark protective history continues to repeat itself and, until safety begins to arise, each person, wisely and creatively, will maintain care for Self by unconscious means.

Consciousness is the path to an ending of suffering, in that that which has had for so long to be hidden can now emerge. The crux is that the raising of consciousness in an individual requires a holding from another which creates a bridge for the individual to emerge. The provision of such holding, and the depth and breadth of it, will depend on the level of consciousness in the person providing the holding. Professional status and title are no guarantee of being able to provide such a safe base for another to emerge. What truly matters is the degree to which the individual has come to know, love and believe in Self and is open to the experience of awe in the presence of another.

A book, a lecture, a friend's story, kindness, support, interest, patience, understanding, compassion, integrity, genuineness, hope – these are some of the experiences that can create a crack in a person's wall of protectors. It is this crack that is the beginning of a letting out of the light of the person's true and precious nature. Breakdowns are really breakthroughs, and the cracking up is a chink of light coming through.

The shift from unconsciousness to conscious care automatically occurs when unconditional love, compassion, understanding and belief in us are present. Naturally, the emergence from behind protective walls can be tentative to begin with; when trust in another has been harshly and continuously belied, caution is a wise and conscious choice. You can always trust yourself; you can always be relied upon to recognise threats to your wellbeing and, depending on the level of safety present, take either protective unconscious steps to reduce the threats or consciously create powerful boundaries to safeguard yourself.

Uncovering The Metaphor Underlying Present Interruptions

In seeking to break out of the protective dance – to use the power of whatever interruption has arisen – it is very important that the protective responses on each person's part are seen as meaningful and purposeful; the protectors are the way in to what it is that lies hidden and is seeking to come into the light of open love. But it needs to be understood that the language of our protectors is metaphorical and their point will be lost unless there is an attempt to read the many layers of the message encapsulated in the metaphor. In the examples below we give some of the possible, real messages underlying common

149

protective communications in interrupted relationships. These are 'possible' underlying messages but it is important to remember that you are the only one who actually knows what it is that is unsayable for you and that has to be buried in the metaphorical message.

A useful way in to what lies hidden in the protective communication is to notice wherever a 'we' or a 'you' occurs and to change it to an 'I'; this brings it back to you and gives you the opportunity to uncover what is going on in your inner world. This is not an easy or simple process because the hidden unsayable truths – for example, "I am a unique, sacred and precious presence in the world", or "my life is given to me for my purposes", or "I am unreservedly deserving of unconditional loving responsiveness to my felt experience of life" – are fundamental and profound. But this is the process that enables real safeguarding of your wellbeing, unlike the impossibility of care that exists when you are focused on a 'you' or a 'we', where you have no information, no firm ground to stand on, and no scope for action.

When you find the safety to stand firmly in your own space, to stand in your own individual presence, substantial, taking your own place in the world, separate in your own right, this brings such a sense of security, possibility, power, liberation, independence, rightness and joy that it makes worthwhile the challenge and effort of going inwards, of reflection, of uncovering.

The truth-telling being called for will differ for each couple. It is in the nature of things that there are three stories to unravel, and the relationship within and between the two individuals is complex, creative and intelligent. The story for both persons is more often one of survival, resulting in the development of a powerful underworld – a hidden cosmos – so that, depending on the threats experienced in our young lives, what we hear and see is the Screen, the mask, rather than what we really need to hear and see in ourselves and in the Other. A literal response to protective and threatening behaviours, either from ourselves or from the Other, only serves to intensify the inner and outer relationship interruptions.

A response that recognises the metaphorical significance of the behaviours – what is surface metaphorically represents a depth of untold suffering – is the only way forward, this being the first essential step to the self-emergence that is the foundation of a real, intimate relationship.

Partners in an interrupted relationship will use different expressions to describe what is happening. For example:

- "We're like ships that pass in the night"

- "We never talk with each other"

- "We never go out together"

- "She's obsessed with the children"

- "He's never at home"

   "There is nothing between us"

- "We're just no longer compatible"

- "She spends more time with her mother than with me"

- "You're married to your work"

- "I can't stand the sight of him anymore"

In these expressions of interruption, the partner making the complaint is being protective, and not at all being plain about what he or she really needs from Self and from the Other. You will recall that what a person says about the Other is entirely about himself or herself; any other interpretation misses the truth of the matter, and the chasm within and between the two people widens. You can guess what the Other's complaints are metaphorically revealing but only the Other can verify your guesses. In any case, when holding is present, it is best that each of you begins to take conscious responsibility for what you feel, think and say because all these experiences are the bridge that brings you home to your hidden Self and, subsequently, out to your partner.

In order to respond proactively to the expressions of the interruption, it is necessary to 'read between the lines' and attempt to unravel what conscious realisations and actions are being called out for yourself that are being captured metaphorically; the message in the metaphor being completely for you and not at all about the Other.

The Metaphor Underlying "We"

Take the complaint "we're like ships that pass in the night". In this complaint there is projection on to 'we'. The possible hidden message for the partner making the complaint is "I'm passing myself by and that is the darkness – 'night' – I need to examine." In regard to the Other in this example, it is a reasonable guess that she or he too is disconnected from Self. The projection on to 'we' is so clever because 'we' has no substance, only individual 'I's have presence; 'we' has no heart and no head and so the relationship stalemate remains. The partner making the complaint can stay in the comfort zone of inaction and can avoid the risk of making himself or herself visible.

But, of course, the complaint is a flag of distress about the fear of being visible in one's own individuality and particularity, and unless the flag is responded to with safety, it will, very sadly, be flown in vain. The amazing truth is that the flags of suffering do continue to get flown; we maintain the hope of being heard at some point. In the relationship interruption being considered here, you might wonder how is it that the other partner is not protesting? Collusion with the shadow 'we' may mean that she or he too is disconnected from her or his presence and it is too risky for her or him to come into consciousness and relate her or his individual story. Be assured that in all troubled and troubling relationships each party has a story that is crying out to be heard.

The road to intimacy with Self and the Other is a long one, but every journey starts with the first step, the first inward step setting the ground for a second step outwards. Taking the present example, imagine what could happen when, let us say, a male partner who unconsciously created the projection becomes conscious of how he needs to begin to meet himself intimately, and to actively create an inner holding of himself; his gaze is now turned inwards and may become a platform – even if a tentative one to begin with – for him to express an unmet need in the relationship with his partner: "I would like to spend time with you and I've booked dinner for us tomorrow night. How does that feel to you?" Notice there is no use of 'we', but a real marking of an 'I' and a 'you'. It may appear a small step but it is a radical shift from the detachment that was there and the unreality of a 'we' to the separateness that is the foundation of intimacy between two individuals.

Obviously, it is not predictable how his partner will respond but, whatever the Other's response, he has certainly begun his journey home to Self. If his partner's response is "I'd like that", then the Other too has taken a first step. If the response should be "Where did that notion come from?" there is a tentative openness to the invitation and the question is a means of checking its genuineness so that it is emotionally safe to take the risk of responding to the invitation. The query certainly opens the door for him to reveal the realisation that is emerging for him and his regrets about not being there for himself and for the Other. A new chapter is opening up for him and possibly for their relationship and, by extension, for the Other also in connecting with Self.

If the Other responds dismissively or in a derisory tone "Where did that idea come from?" then there is now a real challenge for the man to stay grounded, and not step over into the Other's space through personalising the Other's reaction. If he does personalise the Other's reaction, this signals the further inner realisation he needs. If he manages to stay separate, he deepens his own stronghold, and provides a second opportunity for the Other to know him, replying, for example: "I understand your surprise but I have been reflecting and I wish for closer contact with you." This brave new response may take the wind out of the Other's protective sails, who may possibly respond with "Well, well, this is a surprise and worth a try."

In the complaint "we never talk with each other", again there is projection on to 'we', the possible message here being "I don't talk with myself", and a guess for the other partner is "she might be just like myself, fearful of saying what is real."

A realisation that is quite rare is that communication is entirely about getting through to yourself, and any attempts to persuade, blame, or pass the buck of responsibility on to another are clear signs that you are protectively communicating from the outside in rather than from the conscious inside out. In the above couple situation, the partner making the complaint – let us say it is a woman – is unconsciously putting the responsibility for communication on to a non-existent 'we' which cannot initiate any action and thereby avoids risk taking – what a wonderful strategy! If the partner making the complaint were to replace the 'we' with 'I' so that the exclamation is now "I never talk about anything", a truer picture would begin to emerge.

The question that is then begging is: "Do you converse with yourself; do you know what you might like to talk about?" Inner conscious conversations are the solid platform that enables you to let the Other know you in terms of your relationship with yourself and with the Other. It is not anybody's business to read your mind – a not infrequent protective expectation – but it is your business to ensure that the Other knows you. Quite a challenge for any of us, but it is liberating when we wittingly embrace it. If the woman in the present example now begins to listen and respond to herself, she may feel safe enough to reveal: "I have become so conscious of how little I say about what I feel, think and wish for in my relationship with you, this being a painful but enlightening realisation for me."

What a difference consciousness makes! There is no telling how the Other, who has been equally silent, will respond; perhaps the Other will feel touched, or be silent, frightened or aggressive. Clearly, a 'feeling touched' response strengthens the bridge of direct and clear communication that is present – albeit tentative – and creates an opportunity for a heart-to-heart conversation. The three examples of protective responses can be seen as signalling that the Other is operating from the view that 'one swallow doesn't make a summer' – one open expression does not make for a conscious relationship. If the woman in the example can hold herself steady, she may continue to convey something further about herself, such as: "I would like to say a lot more about what I would like to bring to my relationship with you, and understand if you require some time to consider what I am offering."

Whatever the subsequent response from the Other, the hope is that she will persist in deepening her listening to and talking with herself, and follow through on the truths that will emerge of what she deserves from herself and from the Other. If the Other persists with protective responses, she may need to seek outside support for her to continue her inward journey. If she reverts to her protective world, then there is interruption again, and the relationship will go from one silent crisis to another.

The Metaphor Underlying "We Never Go Out Together"

In the complaint "we never go out together", there are projections on to 'we' and 'together'. These projections can bring wonderful opportunities for both individuals in the relationship and what takes place between them but, most of all, the opportunity is for the designer of the projections.

If the complaint were to be taken literally, the focus would be on the absence of the couple's social life and the push would be for action on that lack, such a push being unlikely to lead to any secure, lasting improvement in matters. Taking the complaint as a hidden, metaphorical message about the complainant's inner world, and changing the hollow 'we' to the

'I' of substance, would uncover the call for the complainant to get together with Self and to bring that inner togetherness to the relationship with the Other and to socialising with others. The person making the complaint – let us say it is a woman – may not know the source of the Other's social reticence. It is a good guess that the Other too needs to get together with Self, but she can certainly work on 'getting together' within herself, and then bring that felt experience of 'having it all together' to the Other. If she can do this, without any expectations, the chances are good that her genuine expression of "I would like to spend time going out with you" will be positively met.

If the Other's response is protective, but she does her best to 'keep it together' and reiterates her invitation with, for example, "I would like you to think about my proposal", a shift in consciousness in the Other may also occur. No matter what happens between them, she needs to continue deepening the togetherness within so that the dependence that was there will slowly dissolve and be replaced by what was always present but hidden – her power beyond measure to live her own life, and no longer needing to wait for the Other or insubstantial 'we' to do it for her. If support is not forthcoming to any degree from the Other, it is important she finds it outside the relationship.

The Metaphor Underlying "She's Obsessed With The Children"

A not infrequent complaint from men is that their wives or partners are 'obsessed with the children'. Indeed, there are many women – and some men – who unconsciously live their lives through and for their children. There is great wisdom for the individuals involved in this protective over-caring of children. The wisdom can be that the enmeshment with children points to an underlying 'need to be needed' – a powerful substitute for not being held and loved for one's unique presence.

A second purpose can be to draw attention to what was unsayable and undoable during one's childhood, the hope being that somebody with a high level of consciousness will detect what is going on and offer the holding required for emergence into fullness. Some of these mothers will openly assert that "I live for my children" and, sadly, in our society that particular kind of protective response is praised and reinforced. The realisation seeking to emerge is that to be an effective parent I need to live my own life and create the circumstances for my children to live their own lives. The conscious parent accompanies children in their emergence; unconscious parenting can seriously interrupt that sacred process of emergence.

The father in this situation can often be sidelined – ironically very much in the way the mother was sidelined when a child, thereby creating a very powerful re-enactment. The man who makes the complaint "she's obsessed with the children" is projecting on to his wife, and his challenge is to uncover the underlying hidden message, which can be something like "I'm not in possession of myself." The father can often experience rejection and when he 'puts up with it' and does not 'break the silence' on his suffering, somehow there is now a recurrence of his childhood experience when it would have been too terrifying to speak out about not experiencing being loved.

Sadly, we have come across men who did assert their need to be seen and loved by their partners but their partners did not have the safe holding to turn inwards, and so the marriage fell apart. What these men subsequently realised was that their marriage to themselves needed to become their priority. When this priority is present, then the person *really* is ready for marriage and commitment to the Other. In this situation, it is clear that very serious earlier interruptions in both partners' lives are being re-enacted in their marriage and, tragically, in their relationships with their children. If the mother here is protectively blind to her identification with her children, so too is the father protectively blind to his children's individual presence when he does not express his concerns about how their emergence is being interrupted by the mother's obsession. Only when one of the parents comes into consciousness is there a chance for the occurrence of the multiple interruptions to cease.

The Metaphor Underlying "There Is Nothing Between Us"

How does it come about that two people who in courtship could not wait to be together, after years of marriage come to a place of complaining that "there's nothing between us"?

The complaint suggests that, from the outset, the relationship was co-dependent, with the mutual "I can't wait to see you" metaphorically representing the reality that neither partner sees Self and the romantic liaison being a substitute for the real thing – to belong to Self. One of the magnificent illusions to which many are prone is that 'marriage is going to make me happy' and, painfully, this illusion can be quickly shattered, sometimes within weeks of getting married or choosing to live together. The old saying 'if you want to know me, come and live with me' is apt here – the relationship can become chronically interrupted by the unrealistic expectations of each other. When I bring my emptiness to you, no matter what you do, you cannot fill it – it is a bottomless pit. The fact that the

Other accepts the impossible pact is revelatory of his or her own void within.

When disconnection meets disconnection, conflict inevitably and necessarily occurs, but the connections, the realisations being called for may take a long time to emerge or may stay hidden to the grave. In the complaint "there's nothing between us", the significant projection is that on to 'nothing'. In our practice we have encountered many individuals who declare "I feel nothing for myself" or "I am a nothing." There is no lack of intelligence, creativity or unconscious insight here; indeed, when the person reveals his or her story to us, we are in awe of the survival strategies developed, the most powerful being to adopt the internal stance towards Self of 'I'm unlovable', 'I'm nothing'. To begin to allow any glimpse of lovability would amount to risking re-experiencing the horrors of rejection.

When the individual is asked: "If we had your child Self here and you turned to her (or him) and coldly declared 'I feel nothing for you', how do you think that child would feel?" the immediate reply is "devastated." A follow-on query would be: "And the next time you approach that child, how do you think that child will respond?" and the most frequent response is "the child will avoid me." When we then bring it back to the adult person who in the here and now feels like nothing, and we ask: "How many times did you experience such harsh rejection?" the tears flow and the reply is "innumerable times." The reality then is 'innumerable times bitten, infinite times shy' of ever daring to reach out to another again.

If this were to have been your experience, how could you ever allow yourself to feel anything for yourself and risk feeling you deserve to be loved and cherished? It would simply be too terrifying. The feeling nothing for yourself is an internalisation of the experience of having 'nothing' but rejection from the significant adults in your early life who, tragically, were not able to see 'everything' about your sacred and precious presence. When an individual brings that kind of complete protective repression of Self to marriage, it is only a matter of time before interruptions occur to bring attention to the invisibility within, this coming from the hope that this time the invisibility will be seen and responded to with the love it deserves.

The Metaphor Underlying "He's Never At Home"

A not uncommon complaint by women – and men – about their male partners is "he's never at home" believing quite unconsciously that if only the Other would spend more time at home, all would be well. The projection here is on to 'he' and 'home'. The awakening being called for is to see the 'I' hidden behind the 'he' – "I'm not at home with myself" – and the 'home' in question is the inner home within the person making the complaint. You may find yourself reacting to this understanding and protest that surely the reality is that the Other is never at home, and that this is the problem. If so, of course, this protective response is about you, and for you, but it deserves an explanation of what we are suggesting.

There is no denying that the complaint "he's never at home" may have a literal reality, but it is the underlying metaphorical meaning of the complaint that is the key information that needs to come into consciousness. Yes, the Other being out all the time is a serious interruption to the relationship, but so is the partner's complaint. The query arises: "How is it that the complainant has put up with the situation for so long?" When the complainant can own her or his own response, she or he is coming home to Self and, from that inner homeland, now has the ground from which to assert the need for the Other to be more at home. The encouraging reality is that when the complainant comes to know Self, when she or he comes to consciously feel for Self, feel for the hidden hurts and fears, and recognises the crying-out need to be there for Self, she or he will also begin to feel compassion for the Other, and know that somehow or other neither is she or he at home with Self.

There is now a strong possibility for a deepening of the relationship within both individuals and between the two of them. If the Other is not safe enough to respond to the complainant's newfound consciousness, at least the situation has changed for her or him, and new choices will arise regarding the relationship with Self, and the kind of couple relationship desired and sought.

Be assured there is a story behind the complainant's protective complaint and the Other's behaviour of 'never being at home'. As the painful memories surface for each of them, then the sense and meaning of the limbo nature of their relationship, and possibilities for enrichment, will slowly but surely emerge. The 'rupture' can now turn to 'rapture'.

The Metaphor Underlying "She Spends More Time With Her Mother Than With Me"

Complaints that the Other spends more time with family of origin than with present family come from both women and men, even if more frequently from men. Leaving the nest of family of origin is a struggle for many individuals – both male and female – and the continuity of the enmeshment into adult years, and into the intimate couple relationship, creates major interruption to both the individual realisation of Self, and the conscious blossoming of couple intimacy.

Birds readily fly the nest but, because of parental projections on to children, becoming independent and discovering one's own unique flight path is a very scary prospect for many young people. Yet, flying the nest is one of our most important conscious responsibilities and, when it is not achieved, the fallout for intimate relationship, and any children of the next generation, is serious, there being now an endless repetition of interruptions to the real emergence of Self. From the perspective of the partner enmeshed with family of origin, there are many intelligent rationalisations for the enmeshment:

- ▶ "My mother wouldn't hear of me having a life of my own"
- ▶ "My parents would fall apart if I didn't contact them and visit frequently"
- ▶ "My father needs me to look after him in the face of my mother's impossible demands"
- ▶ "I would feel so guilty if I didn't visit my parents several times a week"
- ▶ "They would be lost without me"

It is not difficult to uncover the real message – the unsayable – in such unconscious rationalisations. By simply substituting 'I' for mother, father or parents, the underlying fears appear:

- ▶ "I wouldn't hear of having a life of my own" – what a tragedy!
- ▶ "I would fall apart if I didn't contact and visit my parents frequently" – what an entrapment!

> ❯ "I need to look after me in the face of my mother's impossible demands" – scary prospect!

> ❯ "I would feel so guilty if I didn't visit my parents several times a week" – the challenge of seeing the guilt as being about my care!

> ❯ "I am lost without me" – terrifying revelation!

The conscious actions that are a real response to the tragedy, entrapment, fear and challenge that are exposed in the realisations above are:

> ❯ "I need to live my own life" – freedom at last!

> ❯ "I need to frequently be in contact with and connect with my own interiority – listening in, paying heed – and belong to myself" – getting to really know myself!

> ❯ "I need to establish definite boundaries – actions for myself – when encountering my mother's impossible demands" – independence beckoning!

> ❯ "I need to be actively involved with my own precious life" – guilt free!

> ❯ "I need to find myself" – an exciting and sacred journey!

When the partner enmeshed with family of origin realises her or his commitment to one's own life, and is able to let go the protective responsibility for one or both parents, such consciousness, while hugely important for her or him, does not resolve the Other's complaint who also has to face his or her projection on to the Other. The question arises for the complainant as to why he or she has put up with the Other's enmeshment with family of origin for all these years. Is it that in some way he or she does not feel worthy of openly asking for the Other's presence and time? More deeply, is the real issue that he or she does not give himself or herself precious time – perhaps therein lies the crux of the complaint? Before realisation, he or she will be convinced that if only the Other changed the marriage would be fine. But nothing is further from the truth – it is the marriage with Self that needs primary attention.

Should you find yourself in this situation, spending time with yourself, being with yourself might mean checking in, and connecting with the felt experience when your life partner is distracted from, and is non-attentive to, the care of your shared life. The call to you is to identify and hold with what is important to you in an intimate relationship – being present to one another, a sense of your couple relationship being the priority relationship, the relationship of primary interest, of primary attention.

The query for you now is can you find the inner safety to initiate talk about all this and, very importantly, can you keep your eye off the Other, and keep looking at what you are doing, or not doing, to safeguard what you consider to be crucial to an intimate relationship? You need to keep taking your cues from yourself, rather than getting lost in an argument or a fight with the Other. You need to stay attentive to what works best for you in how you spend your time, keep being creative about having a happy, satisfying, fulfilling lifestyle, keep putting out the invitation to the Other to join you, and if she or he cannot find the inner safety to join you, you need to continue independently with the life that is right for you.

The Metaphor Underlying "You're Married To Your Work"
The addiction to work is a common phenomenon, frequent among men, and growing in frequency among women. The

word 'addiction' speaks to us of story – a tale where the child's presence was confused with school performance or some other performance such as sports, music, art, caring for others. The higher the achievement, the more recognition received and, cleverly, the child discovered that this substitute recognition was better than no recognition at all. But the addiction to proving oneself through a particular activity is a never-ending pressure because you are only as good as your last performance.

Many men have come to us with the wonderful protective belief 'I am my work', and we have witnessed their terror at any prospect of falling off the pedestal of success they have creatively made for themselves. It is powerful for these men when they come to the conscious realisation that their worth lies in their presence, that their worthiness of love is a given, requiring no proof. As they come to hold precious their own presence, they find themselves spontaneously letting go of the projections on to them from one or both of their parents. When not resolved, this protective dependence on work can have devastating fallout on the person's psychological, social and physical wellbeing, on the person's intimate relationship and, often, there is repetition of the confusion of presence with performance among their children, and in the workplace the presence of unrealistic expectations and threatening management approaches.

In a marriage, it is not the person who is work-addicted who will first point to the protector being played out but the spouse. But what these spouses do not recognise for themselves is that when they make the complaint "you're married to your work", they are projecting on to the Other, and indirectly are talking about themselves – all this, of course, at an unconscious level.

If they were speaking from a place of consciousness, they would send an 'I' message that would express a need of their own, and a compassionate understanding of the Other's work addiction. For example: "I would like more time with you, and I am concerned about the amount of time you give to work and the little time you have for yourself, for me and our children."

A message coming from a separate 'I-land' opens up the space between the two people and allows the possibility of real talk about the unhappy situation; real talk being about the felt experience on both sides. It becomes safer for the work-addicted partner to reflect on the hidden, metaphorical meaning of the addiction, and the other person's wellbeing is also better safeguarded through making himself or herself known in their needs, longings, losses, hopes in the situation.

The complaint "you're married to your work" communicates nothing about the complainants, and the query arises as to the ways in which they themselves are married to their work – whatever the nature of that 'work' might be – which could, for example, be the impossible work of always trying to mind others.

The Metaphor Underlying "I Can't Stand The Sight Of Him Anymore"

The outburst – let us say it is from a wife about a husband – that "I can't stand the sight of him" reveals that the wife has no sight of her own individuality and is bringing her emptiness to the Other, in the hope that he will fill the void within. The husband who struggles with this complaint – for example, trying to defend himself, or argue, or attack back, or try to please – has, of course, also no sight of himself. The repetition of earlier abandonments cuts deep, and the desperation to make the Other responsible is meaningful but is always going to be an impossible agenda, and the intensification of the suffering screams out for each partner to follow the path whereby they find the safety to inhabit their own individuality.

When the partner who makes the complaint comes to that quest with consciousness, certainly it will no longer be a case of "I can't stand the sight of him" but a hope and support for him to catch sight of himself. The emergence of sight of Self is likely to be a long way down the road. For the complainant, the underlying real issue needing to emerge is likely to be something on the lines of "if you do not have sight of yourself, then you cannot have sight of another". For the Other in the situation, the needed reflection is on the felt experience of being exposed to such a protective message from his or her partner. How do you find the holding of yourself, how do you stand for yourself, how do you uphold your worthiness of being seen and loved in the face of what is likely to be a repetition of earlier experiences of invisibility and rejection? Clearly, there are major challenges for both partners in coming through such an interruption.

Finding The Loving Response

Our nature is love, and in each one of us the impetus always is to find a way to express that love. Tragically, the route to open expression of love is almost always blocked for us in one way or another. Instead of being able to rest into, to trust our spontaneously loving expression, we learn that we are not to be trusted as loving beings, and we learn that there are certain prescriptions and proscriptions around the expression of love. One such deviation from spontaneous loving expression that most of us have learned that we must make is to look to what is happening with the Other as the criterion of the ethics, morality, maturity, lovingness of our behaviour. But we are looking the wrong way; the issue is not "am I doing right by the Other, but am I doing right by myself?" How the Other responds to me reflects her or his inner world; for example, I may be behaving in a very loving way by leaving the Other to figure out something for himself or herself, but out of protectiveness the Other may want me to take charge of her or his life and be very rejecting and castigating of me when I do not take on that impossible task.

Likewise, if the Other is in a protective place, he or she may be delighted with me when I sacrifice my life for him or her – but there is no love in that, either for the Other or for me. It can be very challenging to find the truly loving response when you meet protectiveness in the Other. If I am in a protective place myself, I may rush in trying to fix things for the Other; I may leave my own space and intrude myself where I do not belong. I do not have any of the real information about what is happening for the Other – only the Other has that information. If I act as if I know what is going on and what is needed, I am simply projecting my own stuff on to the Other – no real love here now either. If I stay in my own space, notice my own fears and my own protective responses, if I try to stay present to myself and find what is being called for my wellbeing, then I will be in the grounded, steady, secure place that will enable me to be present to the Other – now real love is present for the Other and for me.

Being present – listening, hearing, understanding, 'getting' the Other, respecting separate presence, respecting the Other's own knowing, kindness, empathy, fellow-feeling, compassion – is the ultimate expression of love. You are the one who can do the checking as to whether or not you are present to yourself and to the Other. When you check, you will recognise the felt experience of when you are present – a felt experience of 'rightness', lightness, openness, calm, joy, softness, strength; and the felt experience of when you are gone from yourself – a felt experience of anxiety, tension, heaviness, unsteadiness, hopelessness – very clear criteria for the existence or otherwise of real love.

Waymarkers On The Road To Rapture

Below are noted some of the waymarkers on the road to the rapture that is possible to occur when the safety is there for each individual in the couple to look beneath the presenting rupture for the hidden realisation that needs to emerge for the sake of individual wholeness, wellbeing, all-one-ness.

- *Acknowledgement* that 'the trouble' between us is not the burning issue, it is our inner disconnection from Self that is crying out to be seen and resolved – what a realisation!

- *Understanding* that the relationship interruptions have been unconscious creative attempts to hold on to the couple relationship rather than holding on to self, which has been too terrifying to attempt – such powerful and meaningful creativity!

- *Accepting* that in some marvellous way we found each other in order ultimately to find our own self – magic!

- *Realising* that this partnership arose from the creative realms of the unconscious with the hope of a conscious awakening, the hope of a breakthrough – inspirational!

- *Understanding* that each of our sufferings in the past are being re-enacted in the present context of our troubled relationship, so that what has lain hidden can come to light – enlightening!

- *Seizing* the opportunity in our crisis to connect with Self, and from that solid interiority to connect with each other – opportunity knocks!

- *Finding* compassion for our individual suffering and the suffering of each other – heart-warming!

- *Recognising* that development of conscious trust in Self and in each other requires patient holding – no greater wisdom than kindness!

- *Allowing* the awe of Self and awe of each other to slowly but surely emerge – powerful!

- *Becoming* open to differences between us as sources of creativity rather than being seen as disagreements – peace reigns!

- *Holding* each other's fundamental all-one-ness – guardians of solitude!

- *Seeing* that separateness is the basis for togetherness – oh happy day!

- *Owning* protective reactions and the opportunities these provide for a deepening of the inner relationship with self – the road less travelled!

- *Supporting* each other's inner relationship with Self – coming home!

- *Knowing* that a fulfilling relationship with the Other rests on the degree to which each of us consciously loves Self – this is what relationship is all about!

- *Determining* to stay on the inner path, even in the face of the Other's protective responses – having boundaries!

- *Communicating* directly and openly from the 'I' place about needs, fears, wishes and aspirations – no confusion!

▶ *Hearing* what is not being said and seeing what is not being done by Self and by the Other – clarity of vision!

▶ *Distinguishing* between 'being' and 'falling' in love, open and protective desire, lust and attraction – real love!

When reading through the above waymarkers, any that resonate with you are important starting points. For example, if what stood out for you is that each of us needs to embrace our fundamental all-one-ness, then an exploration of your current level of inhabiting that aloneness, that individuality, undoubtedly will throw light on the need to deepen that essential experience. This may mean a deeper affirming of your uniqueness, your unrepeatable potentiality, your individuality, and power beyond measure to live life from the inside out.

It may also mean revisiting past hurts that creatively and wisely led you to disconnect from your true nature, allowing the fears, hurts and humiliations to rise to the surface and for you, now as an adult, to listen and comfort yourself, and to reassure that child-hurt within that you now see and embrace your true and awesome Self. If you find yourself struggling to do this, it may be that a safe place is being called for – with friend, sibling, colleague, therapist. Only you know what it is you need to seek, but be assured that there are people there who care.

Maybe what resonates for you is that no threatening behaviour towards one another ever had the intention of hurting; the unconscious intention always being to protect yourself from a repeat of the abandonment experiences of childhood. The heart softens when this realisation comes into consciousness. Furthermore, the responsibility to be there for yourself strengthens, and the resolve deepens to create boundaries – not walls – in the face of the protective responses of the Other. There is a profound difference between 'feeling sorry' for the Other and having compassion. 'Feeling sorry' can frequently lead to taking care of the Other, which protectively serves the provider – a need to be needed perhaps – while compassion has no hidden agenda. Compassion is empathic but also empowering in that it supports the Other to take conscious responsibility for his or her own life.

We have no doubt that each person who is troubled or troubling wants to get together with the Other in all the rapturous ways described above. The human spirit is love and, when uninterrupted in its expression, will bring all the above and more to the Other. But when any of us has experienced harsh interruptions to Self-expression, coming out from behind the powerful walls of our protectors requires predictable and immense safe holding. To paraphrase the government of Bhutan: the future of society rests not on 'gross national productivity' but on 'gross national consciousness of our true nature'.

Chapter Nine

Where Do I Go From Here?

Relationship With Yourself: The Only Way To Go

When there are interruptions in the intimate relationship, you may find yourself asking "where do I go from here?" this query usually being interpreted as "should I stay or leave the couple relationship?" But whatever happens with your coupledom, there is really only one way for you to go and that is towards relationship with yourself. You have seen that the resolution of interruptions rests with each partner becoming consciously aware, and taking conscious actions, primarily around how each relates to Self, and from that solid interiority, around how each relates to the Other.

Contrary to popular thinking, each partner is responsible for his or her own wellbeing, and when each partner is conscious of that reality, they will support each other on that essential inner quest. The opposite is also true: when neither partner has come to conscious ownership for their individual lives, then interruptions necessarily and creatively arise from the unconscious 'comfort zones' of both – a suffering that is signalling hidden selves.

The question "where do I go from here?" in the face of intimate couple interruptions is a critical one, because whether or not the couple relationship comes into harmony, the pursuit of each partner's relationship with Self needs to be continued – to death's door! The answer you give to this question is crucial for your wellbeing. The decision to stay or leave the interrupted relationship is not the critical direction at stake; whether you stay or leave, where you always need to be headed is towards a harmonious relationship with yourself – headed towards wholeness, fullness, all-one-ness.

It certainly is good news, and it certainly is possible, when in following the direction of a loving relationship with Self, and the Other doing likewise, that you are able to realise the potential of the interruptions that have occurred, and reach a place of real intimacy and harmonious journeying together. This kind of outcome requires strong safe holding, the kind of holding that very sadly is often absent in our family, community and societal worlds. The safe holding exists but you may have to make efforts to seek it out and find it.

Many couples do not find the safe holding that enables both partners to adopt conscious responsibility for their separate lives whereby they can co-operate in the building of shared living that encompasses separateness and togetherness. In the absence of safe holding, individuals may settle for some degree of comfort rather than fullness – for all sorts of reasons, conscious and unconscious. For example: a couple may reach some compromise that enables them to stay together 'for the children's sake'; or the couple may stay in the relationship for financial reasons but have separate bedrooms and go on few social outings together; or the couple may maintain an outward coupledom and establish some degree of co-operation between them; or a couple may stay together for 'religious reasons' or in order not to upset the family of origin.

At all outward levels – practical, social, financial and family – leaving is a complex business, and it becomes even more intricate when you consider what lies hidden. Whether a person decides to compromise and be happy with 'a half rather than a full loaf' of a couple relationship, the maintenance and deepening of the relationship with Self is still the priority. Support for that inner relationship is unlikely to be strongly present in an intact but unhappy relationship, or where the couple are separated or divorced, but supports are available beyond the marriage and family of origin. Where a partner settles for less than the fullness of real intimacy, enhancement of the relationship with Self is essential because challenges are definitely going to arise to test the unstable apparent stability. It seems that this is often even more true for couples living apart, especially where the couple have children.

A Relationship With Yourself: What Does That Mean?

A question that frequently arises is: "What does it mean to have a loving relationship with yourself?" It can seem sentimental, unreal, 'just words' but, actually, when you check you will find that the relationship with yourself is a very real, energetic and powerful experience. You know, for example, the felt experience of when you are harassing yourself, being judgmental, rejecting and mean towards yourself, and you know the difference between that experience and the felt experience that comes with you being understanding, compassionate, honouring and generous towards yourself.

Essentially, a loving relationship with yourself comprises all those behaviours – internal and external – that safeguard your unique, sacred and precious presence in the world.

In your intimate couple relationship, the nature of your relationship with yourself colours your answers to such queries as: "Where do I end and the Other begin?" "Where can we meet?" "How can I 'be with' rather than 'be for' the Other?" The following sections spell out how you might be with yourself in all the expressions of Self in a way that reflects an emergence into the fullness and particularity of who you are in your unique presence.

Safeguarding Your Wellbeing

If bringing the fullness of your presence to the Other is the key to real intimacy, then the question arises as to how you find that fullness in yourself. You have seen (Chapter Three) how in our early lives, and continuing into adulthood and present lives, we can experience interruptions to any of the expressions of Self – emotional, social, physical, sexual, intellectual, behavioural and creative – and we learn to hide aspects of ourselves in the face of such interruptions. It is not that the fullness of who we are has been diminished or damaged or tarnished; it is always there but has had to be buried, the effort now being to find the safety to let it emerge again. It is a matter of refinding – rediscovering – rather than finding.

Conscious awareness is what turns the key to the spaciousness of open, free, full, spontaneous expression of yourself. When you reflect on what you actually received and on what you would have loved and longed for in regard to the different expressions of Self, then you know what responsiveness is being called for by you towards yourself; you know what new choices, decisions, actions are being called for in the interests of your wellbeing.

Your Felt Experience: The Key Information For Your Wellbeing

Your felt experience is the key information in finding responsiveness. You know the felt experience when there is neglect, abandonment, rejection, and you can begin to know the felt experience of loving care, of unconditional regard and respect for your unique, sacred and precious presence in the world. Your felt experience is the criterion for whether you are surviving or thriving, whether you are in a state of distress or of wellbeing. Sadly, we are often deprived of access to that vital information because it has not been allowed to us; checking in with ourselves has not been encouraged and our experience has not been responded to when we did express it. The saying 'the operation was a success but the patient died' captures what is not an uncommon experience.

Take, for example, the student who gets straight 'A's in all examinations but nobody enquires: "So what was school life like for you?" If that query had been made, the answer might very well have been: "I was stressed, I missed out on so much of what my friends were doing, I was afraid all the time of not achieving the high grades expected of me." The message the student gets in the hugely important holding worlds of home, school, community and society is that performance trumps experience.

Another example is the husband who fulfils all expectations in regard to creating a successful business, providing a lovely home and financial security for his family and who, to everyone's dismay, becomes depressed and apathetic. The depression and apathy are the wake-up call for him to check with himself what the living of that success story has been like for him – "who was there?" – was it his Real Self or his Screen Self? Was he acting in a way that was right for him, that was fulfilling for him, or was he acting in accordance with expectations, demands, goals of others? Was he acting from the outside in rather than from the inside out?

What a terrible message to receive that it does not really matter how you are finding life so long as you live up to expectations, when the truth is that the quality of your lived experience in the world outweighs all other considerations. The irony is that when that truth is upheld, this is when we are safe to give of the best of ourselves, and when we are most likely to realise the wonderful intelligence, capability and creativity that are part and parcel of our human nature.

Every Hair On Your Head Is Counted

There is a phrase from the Bible, intended to capture the extent of God's love for human beings, that is the perfect metaphor for the loving responsiveness towards yourself that is necessary and worthy of you: "every hair on your head is counted". The phrase implies attention to detail – the detail of your felt experience, the detail of the quality of the experience of your everyday life. If in your early life you had had the kind of relationships that conveyed to you that 'every hair on your head is counted', then you would have had the security that enables you to be fully alive, fully active in the world, fully expressive of your individual Self. You would know that you are going to be OK no matter what life throws up for you, no matter the things that turn up over which you have no control: illness, loss, accident, failure.

It is our human tragedy that none of us gets that loving message completely. In fact, what we most often get is the opposite: it gets conveyed to us that acting out of the place that our lived experience matters is bad, selfish, and will call down on us disapproval, rejection, punishment. These are experiences that, as children, cause us terror and which we will do anything to avoid; we will try to live our lives for others, we will abandon and neglect ourselves in the name of 'unselfishness'. The dissonance between what we know in our wisdom to be the truth – "I am always deserving of unconditional loving responsiveness" – and what we are finding in our holding worlds is too great to sustain as children and so we bury the truth until the time comes when there is sufficient safety to let it begin to emerge.

It can feel like a very big risk to start acting as if the quality of your lived experience actually matters, but it is in taking that risk, in whatever small ways to begin with – for example, making a real choice about what you would like for your supper, as opposed to having whatever is in the fridge – that the internal evidence begins to build up that this is the route to living fully, to having a zest for life, to having optimism. When you realise this truth for yourself, then, of course, this is also what you will bring to the Other, and you will find yourself supporting and encouraging him or her to also act out of the loving place where 'every hair on your head is counted'.

Returning To The Truths Of Who You Really Are

Your presence in the world gets expressed through the different and amazing channels: physical, sexual, emotional, social, intellectual, behavioural and creative. A powerful way to create safety for emergence from being hidden to being fully present is to return to and ground yourself in the truths of who we really are in our human presence in the world. Grounding yourself in these truths enables you to shift from an unconscious unloving stance towards yourself (being hidden) to a stance that is loving, kind, respectful, caring and emerging into the light.

Physical and Sexual Truths

- My body is a vehicle for life; it does the job perfectly irrespective of shape, size, colour or appearance

- My body is powerfully attractive as a living presence

- My body is sacred – always deserving of care, respect, dignity, honouring

- My body is fundamentally right in itself – distinct, unrepeatable

- My body has wonderful pleasure-giving capacities – independent of outward physical appearance

- My body is a wonderful resource to be cherished

- My body is mine – here for my joy, aliveness, pleasure

Physical and Sexual Emergence

From	To
Carelessness	Care, nurturing
Disconnected	Connected
Performance	Experience
Pleasing others	Pleasing Self
Using for hidden ends	Enjoying for itself
Vehicle for others	For own sake
Mechanical	Cherishing
Dismissing	Appreciating
Rejection	Honouring
Harshness	Friendliness

▶ Crudeness	Respect
▶ Ignorance	Knowing
▶ Ignoring	Listening in
▶ Fighting against	Responsiveness

Emotional Truths

- ▶ Emotions are the truest barometer of quality of life/wellbeing/aliveness
- ▶ Powerful information
- ▶ It is right and good that I tune into my emotions, listen, pay heed
- ▶ My feelings come from me, are about me and are for me
- ▶ Others' feelings come from Others, are about Others and are for Others
- ▶ Emotions call for motion
- ▶ Emotions never lie

Emotional Emergence

From	To
▶ Ignoring	Owning, paying heed
▶ Dismissing	Taking account of
▶ Ridiculing	Taking seriously
▶ Repressing	Taking as cues for action
▶ Fighting against	Opening up to
▶ Struggling with	Embracing
▶ Being bland	Being heartfelt

Social Truths

- I'm one of a kind and special, unrepeatable
- My presence matters
- My absence matters
- I have my own particular place in the world
- It is right and good for me to take my place
- I make a difference in the world by being here
- I have the power to attract others to me by my presence
- I deserve unconditional relating; I am worthy of relationship
- Relationship with others is integral to my humanness

Social Emergence

From	To
Conforming	Following my own lights
Staying hidden	Being communicative
Retiring	Taking my place
Pushy	Staying in my own space
Overwhelming	Allowing difference
Anxious	Grounded
Invisibility	Making myself known

Intellectual Truths

- Each of us has genius
- I am immensely intelligent
- I am always making sense of my world
- I always know the level of threat/safety in my world
- My intelligence gets expressed in a myriad of ways
- Knowledge/examination results are no index of my intelligence
- My intelligence is always at work – even if unconsciously

Intellectual Emergence

From	*To*
Diminishing	Appreciating
Ignoring	Responding to
Hiding	Making visible
Avoiding mistakes	Taking the chance
Pursuing success	Seeking fulfilment
Deferring to others	Holding with my own knowing
Seeing others as the experts	Seeing myself as the expert on me

Behavioural Truths

- All behaviour makes sense
- All behaviour is meaningful – even if at an unconscious level
- I am immensely capable; I am an active agent in my life
- I never intend to be troublesome or to cause pain

Behavioural Emergence

From	*To*
Analysis	Experiencing
Judgment	Understanding
Caution	Trust
Wariness	Spontaneity
Apathy	Active care
Dependence	Independence
In the Other's space	In my own space
Control	Boundaries
Action against others	Action for Self

> ❱ Fending off others   Staying with myself
> ❱ Struggling with others   Safeguarding myself

Creative Truths
> ❱ My creativity is always present – either consciously or unconsciously

> ❱ My power to creatively respond to my world is awesome

> ❱ Relationship with others is the most powerful stimulus . to creativity

> ❱ Open, conscious co-creation with another is one of our . deepest sources of joy

Creative Emergence

From	To
❱ Surviving	Living
❱ Conformity	Individuality
❱ Restriction	Spontaneity, expansiveness
❱ Burdened	Lively, energetic
❱ Pessimistic	Optimistic
❱ Fear	Fearlessness
❱ Narrowness	Open to the vastness of who I am

Telling It Like It Is

A very important part of finding responsiveness towards ourselves, of emerging from being hidden into the open, is being able to recognise, acknowledge and openly declare for ourselves how things actually are in our lives. It is a strange and tragic reality that 'telling it like it is' for many people is undoable. Even at times of serious distress, we can find ourselves diluting the seriousness of the experience: "I'm all right, I'm all right really"; or being very hesitant: "I think, I'm not sure, but something awful might have just happened"; or we excuse the other's behaviour: "I know you didn't mean it, it's just me really, but is there any chance you wouldn't do that?" Or we may react in the opposite fashion and bombard the Other, become aggressive and overwhelming in our behaviour: "you'll stop that right now, if you know what's good for you"; "you bloody bastard"; "you're an absolute disgrace"; "who'd want to put up with the likes of you?"

All these reactions reflect the threats experienced in earlier life in our different holding worlds – particularly in our homes and schools – against openly speaking the truth of our experience. It would be unthinkable, for example, for you as a child to declare to a parent who is being harshly critical: "I am deeply upset by your behaviour, I know I don't deserve it, and I leave it back with you where it belongs." Yet that is precisely the truth of the situation. Because, as a child, you cannot say the truth of how it is for you, you have to bury the experience, and no care happens for you around it; you are left with all the hurt, dismay, confusion, outrage, pain that have arisen for you – there is abandonment of you now. You then come to adulthood, and to the intimate couple relationship, with a fear of letting yourself be known and the dread of further abandonment experiences.

If intimacy is to flourish, it becomes crucial that you start finding the safety to 'tell it like it is' – the most important person to hear and receive the message now being yourself – so that whatever loving responsiveness is being called for in the situation can be put in place by you. This is how you can bring your fullness to the intimate couple relationship. It is crucial for your wellbeing that you be able consciously to see, recognise, identify, acknowledge, allow what is happening in you because that is the pertinent information which when used to guide your actions, choices and decisions – internal and external – leads to real care of you. There is such relief when you can face into and give expression to your actual felt experience; the relief flagging that a profound act of love is taking place now, unlike the child's situation where you were dependent on your parents or other significant adults to do the caring needed.

Chapter Ten

Have I Found What I'm Looking For?

The Quest For The Sacred Marriage

So far, this book has been concerned with the interruptions that can arise in our everyday relationships – with ourselves and with Others – and about using the opportunities provided by those interruptions to break through to a greater conscious, loving connection with ourselves and with those Others with whom we are seeking intimate coupledom. The desire for intimate connection with the Other is worthy of the challenge, reflection, commitment of time and effort involved; real connection being precious with all the joy, warmth, and sense of aliveness and fulfilment it can bring. But in following this pathway of conscious, real connection, we have come to realise that there is a longing in us that is even more profound than the psychological longing for intimacy with the Other. There is a longing for what we are calling the 'sacred marriage' which is a spiritual longing, a longing for transcendent unity, for unity with the Source of all that is. Ultimately, the union between Self and Spirit is the true and sacred marriage for which we all long.

Certainly, when you make the breakthrough to a conscious togetherness with yourself, and intimacy with the Other, glimpses of realisation of this deeper longing emerge; there is an experience of deep peace that surpasses all understanding. This felt experience of oneness with self, of oneness with the Other, of oneness with all that is, we have had in the co-creational therapeutic relationship, and in silent contemplation. There occurs a sense of the Divine within, and a connection to the presence of the Divine – no matter how fleeting – which reason cannot comprehend, but the felt experience is most definitely spiritual in nature. Indeed, it is our experience that love of Self and of the Other is a powerful pathway to that deeper spiritual experience. The spiritual experience is greatly facilitated when you consciously emerge from behind the protective walls you wisely erected as a child, and continued to erect into adult years.

Relationship interruption – with yourself or with the Other – is the ally that calls for not only psychological but also spiritual breakthrough. Everybody benefits when you embrace your all-one-ness, and when you determine to live your own life fully and compassionately. We believe more glimpses of realisation of this deeper longing are possible when the safe holding is present to prioritise our inner course, and embrace the compassionate, non-judgmental reflection that enables us to come home more to our true nature.

A Sense Of Spirit

In this final chapter of the book we present what, in our psychological investigations, has emerged for us as indicators of Spirit, and we invite you to consider whether any of these resonate for you as you undertake the psychological reflections that comprise all the earlier chapters of the book. In his book *The Eden Project,* James Hollis[10] writes beautifully of resonance:

---

[10] Hollis, James. *The Eden Project. In Search of the Magical Other.*
Toronto: Inner City Books, 1998

"Activation of the psychic tuning fork within tells us that soul is present. Like calls to like. The principle of resonance tells us what is of us, about us, for us, even as it retains its mystery." If something in what we say here resonates with you, there will be the thrill and excitement of recognition – the thrill and excitement that come when something hits you in your core.

Of course, this experience of resonance arises only because you already have an inner knowing of the truth of the matter, even if you have had to keep that knowing at an unconscious level. Safety within yourself, and in your relationships with Others, lets that knowing emerge into the open. As you have seen, your Self recognises when threat is present, and when there is threat will keep the knowing in the unconscious, and when there is safety your Self will bring the knowing into consciousness. This knowing in your core, and the making of the choice as to whether to keep the knowing hidden or bring it into the open is, for us, a key index of the existence of Spirit.

Love Is Always Present

Reflection on the power – through the breakthroughs that can occur – of the interruptions that arise in our relationships brings us into contact with the extraordinary and ever-present wisdom, powered by love, that is our nature. The giving and receiving of unconditional love is our natural home; the home in which we are always seeking to rest, either openly and consciously or protectively and unconsciously. As infants, we have a knowing that our being is love and, unless interruptions occurred in the womb world, spontaneously reach up to give and receive love. Tragically, through the experience of relationship interruptions, we learn to be wary of spontaneous expressions of our love, but that love is always present.

We actually never cease to love ourselves! If you had not undertaken the kind of conscious reflection that has been the subject matter of all the earlier chapters of this book, you might find this statement hard to swallow in the face of all the wars, political conflicts, social injustices, violence, aggression, avarice, suffocation of individuality, illness, corruption, fanaticism, passivity, self-harm, suicide that we read about daily or experience directly in our own lives.

Yet, as you have seen, all of these actions are perpetrated only by those who have had unconsciously to become disconnected from Self and who, in the face of rejection of their presence, valiantly and creatively form a Screen or Shadow Self. This Shadow Self comprising all the protective behaviours, emotions, thoughts, attitudes and creative strategies through which we have cleverly learned to manage the threatening worlds which we can find ourselves inhabiting. Every protective response is an act of love because, as you have seen, its purpose is to guard the pearl of great price, the individual and sacred presence that is each one of us. Nobody with conscious holding of their precious and sacred presence would perpetrate threatening reactions towards themselves or towards others.

It is awesome to see that our loving wisdom is always present – whether we are thriving or striving, depressed or feeling alive, ill or healthy, always seeking the best that can be done in a human world of threat, pain and suffering. Out of love, your Self is always noticing, bearing witness, paying heed, responding to how things are in your different holding worlds, finding the best care when there are threatening circumstances. This love is above and beyond the finite love we may have the blessing to find in intimate relationship with the Other; it is a love that is always present, persistent, pervasive, infinite.

To know and experience such love consciously is our deepest quest in our human existence. If we accept that the Self is love and that each protective response is an act of love – a concealing of presence in circumstances of threat and terror – then the question arises as to whence this amazing phenomenon comes. Kneeling at the altar of our creative protectors is a first conscious step towards coming to the realisation that 'we are already what we are seeking'; our birthright is not only to be home with Self and with the Other, but also with the source of our being – Absolute Love.

The Deeper Knowing That We Possess

As alluded to above, one of the amazing aspects of our human nature is the presence of an underground stream of knowing – a guiding motif – a knowing that has no need of outside information. It is present whether we are experiencing great joy or the depths of despair. This mysterious knowing – described by Housden[11] as "a flash from some other domain that is an intrinsic part of the human experience" – implies a perfection in the way things are. It is this knowing that underlies the truth, referred to many times in earlier chapters, that 'you always are where you need to be'. You always know – even if at an unconscious level – how things are in your world, and what has to be done to protect your presence, and help you withstand the protective responses you meet with in Others. We know the truth of who we are – unique, sacred and precious presences in the world – and we know what is worthy of us, and we hold with those truths through darkness, through our protectors, and through light, through open expression.

---

[11] Housden, Roger. *Ten Poems to Change Your Life*. London: Hodder and Stoughton, 2003, p. 14

The source of our human suffering is the fact that the profound truth of who we are – unique, precious and sacred presences, whose driving force is love – is not upheld from the first moments we come into the world. We know the truth of who we are but it is the nature of the human condition that as babies, infants, children we are utterly dependent on the significant adults in our lives – most especially our parents – to mirror that truth back to us. When that mirroring does not occur wholeheartedly and utterly – as it cannot do because our parents are human beings with their own stories of less than complete unconditional love – then the extreme disconnection between the experience of what we are receiving and what we know to be worthy of us causes profound suffering.

What is awesome – awesome because we seem to be able to transcend the human condition – is that we always find ways of managing that tragedy, of enduring the suffering, of surviving, until the time comes when we know it is safe to safeguard ourselves rather than managing others, to withstand rather than endure, to live rather than survive. Our loving knowing is always present, always creatively seeking ways to keep the pain manageable. The light of loving knowing is always present within, even when we feel the world, and life, to be dark and dangerous. This we might indeed call our 'God-like' nature that always knows the state of play in our holding worlds and that always finds the response that will keep us afloat in the face of what can often be experienced as an ocean of threat. Of course, the deeper guiding vision of our loving knowing is to return home to the place of truth, this being the place where there is an end to suffering, the place where we can rest in unconditional love.

Each one of us shares in the two-sided human condition – the experience of suffering and the spacious loving knowing that holds it all – and it is this that connects us to one another, that brings forth understanding, compassion, and a sense of being fellow travellers. The Real Self – that creates the Shadow Self so that we may be able to live in our human world – in its wisdom, in its abiding love, in its ever-present knowing, joins us with something greater, something deeper, more expansive than our human psychology: it joins us to the community of Spirit.

Our Awesome Creativity

As co-creational travellers in our work with Others, we never cease to be amazed at the wondrously creative ways of either surviving or thriving that individuals find for themselves. Indeed, it is often in the face of such creativity that we experience a sense of awe, a sense of something bigger, a sense of oneness with the Other that connects with an even deeper oneness with all that there is. No words can do justice to this experience – it is an experience beyond cognition   but it is a timeless moment and provides a glimpse of the infinity of love and the Self.

In the reflections suggested in earlier chapters you will, perhaps, have come in contact with a sense of that awesome creativity that each of us exhibits, particularly through the protective strategies you will have devised in circumstances of threat, but also through the metaphorical language you create that can encapsulate layers of meaning concerning crucial matters that you dare not express straightforwardly and directly. Our dreams too are wondrous expressions of creativity – tailor-made for our wellbeing. How does it happen that in our dreams we find the exact image that will capture whatever felt experience is causing us suffering but which we are too fearful of expressing openly and directly? Dreams provide an ongoing overview of what is going on in our lives and often reveal the solutions to ongoing suffering. Dreams are, indeed, an amazing gift from the Spirit within.

For us, encountering that creativity, that mysterious ever-present knowing, brings us into connection with something that transcends our ordinary human existence. In a culture that is so consumed with externals, these experiences are resounding evidence for the depths of an inner life.

Resources

Books by Tony Humphreys and Helen Ruddle

Finding Sexual Realness

The Compassionate Intentions of Illness

Understanding Teenagers: Sometimes Wild, Always Wise

Relationship, Relationship, Relationship:
The Heart of a Mature Society

Books by Tony Humphreys

Leadership with Consciousness

Self-Esteem, the Key to Your Child's Future

Leaving the Nest: What Families are all About

The Power of 'Negative' Thinking

Myself, My Partner

Work and Worth: Take Back Your Life

A Different Kind of Discipline

Whose Life are you Living?

Examining Our Times

The Mature Manager: Managing from Inside Out

All About Children: Questions Parents Ask

CDs by Tony Humphreys

Raising Your Child's Self-Esteem
Self-Esteem for Adults
Work and Self

Book titles with Helen Ruddle

O'Connor J., Ruddle, H. and O'Gallagher, M., *Caring for the Elderly, Part II: The Caring Process: A Study of Carers in the Home*

O'Connor J., Ruddle, H. and O'Gallagher, M., *Cherished Equally? Educational and Behavioural Adjustment of Children*

O'Connor J. and Ruddle, H., *You Can Do It: A Life Skills Book for Women*

O'Connor J., Ruddle, H. and O'Gallagher, M., *Sheltered Housing in Ireland: Its Role and Contribution in the Care of the Elderly*

O'Connor J. and Ruddle, H., *Business Matters for Women*

O'Connor J. and Ruddle, H., *Breaking the Silence, Violence in the Home: The Woman's Perspective*

Ruddle, H., *Strengthening Family Communication to Prevent Misuse of Alcohol and Drugs: An Evaluation Study*

Ruddle, H., Donoghue, F. and Mulvihill, R., *The Years Ahead: A Review of the Implementation of its Recommendations*

Ruddle, H. and Mulvihill, R., *Reaching Out: Charitable Giving and Volunteering in the Republic of Ireland – The 1997/98 Survey*

Ruddle, H., Prizeman, G. and Jaffro, G., *Evaluation of Local Drugs Task Force Projects:*

Ruddle, H., Prizeman, G., Haslett, D., Mulvihill, R. and Kelly, E., *Meeting the Health and Social Services Information Needs of Older People*

About the Authors

Tony Humphreys

Dr Tony Humphreys is a Consultant Clinical Psychologist, author and national and international speaker. He began his career as a Clinical Psychologist in State Psychiatric and Psychological Services in England and Ireland and since 1990 has been working in private practice in Ireland. His practice involves working with individuals, couples, families, schools, local communities and the business community.

He is a course designer and director of two courses on communication and self-realisation and relationship mentoring in University College, Cork. He is also a regular guest lecturer in other third level colleges, corporate organisations, wellness groups and educational systems both in Ireland and internationally, including several European countries, Turkey and South Africa.

He is author of many books on practical psychology.

Helen Ruddle

Dr Helen Ruddle is a Psychologist with two main strands to her work-life. Presently her work primarily is with individuals in private practice along with university-level programme development and authorship of books.

She is co-founder with Dr Humphreys of the Irish Association of Relationship Mentors. Earlier in her career she was engaged in research in social policy and was a co-founder of the Policy Research Centre in the National College of Ireland.

She is a prolific author and has co-authored several books with Dr Humphreys.